Freedom from Fear

Freedom from Fear

Overcoming Anxiety
through Faith

Marci Alborghetti

Freedom from Fear
Overcoming Anxiety through Faith
by Marci Alborghetti

Edited by Gregory F. Augustine Pierce
Cover design by Tom A. Wright
Typesetting by Desktop Edit Shop, Inc.

Published by: ACTA Publications
                 5559 W. Howard Street
                 Skokie, IL 60077
                 800.397.2282
                 www.actapublications.com

Library of Congress Number: 2001098294

ISBN: 978-0-87946-231-4

Printed in the United States of America

Year: 06 05 04 03 02
Printing: 7 6 5 4 3 2 1

Contents

Dedication

For God, who daily offers to free me from fear;
to Charlie, for understanding on the days when
I can't seem to accept the offer.

Introduction

For as long as I can remember, I've been worried. Some of my earliest memories are of tossing and turning in my narrow child's bed, unable to sleep, as every fear known to childhood paraded through my little brain. I would watch the line of light under my door, taking a little comfort in this sure sign that my parents were still awake. Until it went off. And then I would clutch a big, blue, one-eyed teddy bear to my stomach, trying to banish my fears until I fell into exhausted sleep.

My poor beleaguered mother would sometimes let me come out and lie on the couch, urging me, "Just try to think about nice things." I tried. I would picture the little hotel at Cape Cod where we stayed one week every summer or the beach where my sister and I took swimming lessons. But my child's mind would always turn to fearsome things. The vision of Cape Cod became worry that we wouldn't be able to go this year because of bad weather. The serene scene of our town beach turned into a chaotic vision of my little sister facedown in the water before I could reach her.

Eventually I learned to cope. When Mom assured me that a catch in my side or a stomachache was a "growing pain," I tried to believe her. When my father would swim out into deep water at the beach, I'd close my eyes until he'd come back safely. As I grew up, I had what I think of as a reverse—or perhaps, perverse—reaction to fear. I took chances. If Dad told me to watch the gas gauge in the car, I'd deliberately drive until it was on empty. Big test tomorrow? I'd be watching TV instead of studying. I skipped classes to take early shifts at my job and walked home during study halls. When I had the chance to live in a safe on-campus dormitory, I took an apartment in the middle of what was euphemistically termed a "challenged" city neighborhood.

In other words, I never learned to deal with fear. I wallowed in it. I fled from it. But deal with it? No. That was too hard. It took the distinct and glowing revelation that fear is displaced only by faith for me to confront my fears, and then I did so only with a supreme and ongoing effort.

I'd taken but a few small steps on the path from fear to faith when my new doctor called me late one night with lab results: "You have malignant melanoma." This is the most serious of the skin cancers, the one that can kill. These and myriad other thoughts started ricocheting around my brain even before I hung up the phone. Shattered, I spent the night curled on the wood floor of my office as my computer chirped away. I was once again the eight-year-old child, watching fearfully through the night. Except this time there was no big, blue teddy bear. That morning I committed myself in earnest to a journey from fear to faith. I've been sidetracked more often than I'd care to admit, but I'm still on the journey and I'd like to share it with you.

One thing I've learned is that traveling from fear to faith may first require a period of standing still. This silent, still time is needed to honestly evaluate where fear comes from. Many of us who live in fear consider ourselves unworthy of fearlessness and therefore fear becomes an integral part of our lives. This fear can be related to how we see or "image" God. If we've been taught to view the divine as the Ultimate Punisher, standing sternly in heaven with a balance sheet of our sins and kindnesses, we've been taught to fear the punishment God might now—or someday—mete out.

To move away from fear as a lifestyle, we must move away from the image of God as Angry Guardian. Reimaging God offers many lovely, hopeful and true possibilities: God as Healer, God as Loving Parent, God as Spirit-with-us, God as Forgiver, God as Stronghold, God as Haven, God as Protector, God as Redeemer, God as Joy-giver, God as Grace-giver, God as Constant Companion. The list is endless, and to honestly eradicate fear, all these wondrous images must be considered.

On the human, day-to-day level, we all live *with* fear. But some of us live *in* fear every moment, every day. Some worries make sense. The fear that your child may run out into the road leads you to teach her to stay in the yard or on the sidewalk. Anxiety about a nagging pain leads you to get a much overdue checkup. Worry about driving on icy roads leads you to avoid unnecessary jaunts and thereby avoid a possible accident.

But when does fear cross the line? When does it become a debilitating or even crippling influence? When does it overshadow faith and destroy common sense? When does it become an obstacle to opportunity and joy? When does it constrain and damage relationships?

At some point for most of us, fear does cross that line. For some, the cause is situational. A recession causes you to lose your job, and fear of failure and financial straits comes charging into the breach. A spouse begins acting distant, and you become consumed with fear about the reason for the change and the future of your life together. A small pain persists, and you begin to imagine the start of a fatal illness. For others, fear is a constant presence. Not a day goes by without us having fearful thoughts of losing a loved one, of poverty, illness, abandonment. For us, *every* situation offers the prospect of tragedy.

In addition to our private fears, the national trauma caused by the September 11, 2001 terrorist attacks on the United States and subsequent events has made unresolved fear part of our common experience, one that we will have to learn to cope with as a people.

Whether you are troubled by occasional worry or constant fear, however, there are ways to cope. Faith is the ultimate antidote, but you may need to reimage God and reexamine or even redefine your faith if you are to be fully girded in the war against fear and anxiety. The reflections, prayers and exercises in this book can help. These selections incorporate the experiences of people who have struggled with fear and moved toward faith. In some cases, you will immediately identify with the situation described; in others, you may be able to use the experience as a model for your own journey from fear to faith. With faith, grace and some effort, we all can learn to "be not afraid."

Decidedly *Not* in Control

My own biggest personal fear is losing my husband. Whether he dies first or I die first doesn't really matter; I'm terrified of being separated from him by *either* death. This terror leads to any number of smaller anxieties which exacerbate this central, consuming fear. I worry about meetings that keep him out late, pushing his normal twelve-hour day to fifteen or sixteen hours. I worry about him commuting in bad weather. I worry when he's sick. I worry when he's in the sun too long. I worry when he goes out on our little Boston Whaler alone. You name it—I'll find a way to turn most any concern into serious anxiety.

Needless to say, this tendency of mine does not enhance our relationship, particularly because my husband is about the calmest and most unruffled person imaginable. Still, my small fears serve an important purpose for me. By focusing on multiple superficial worries, I can avoid dealing with my very real fear of being without Charlie. I find relief in targeting the issues I think I can control, and that false sense of security helps keep the real terror at bay. If I'm nagging him about driving to work on icy roads or reminding him to keep a doctor's appointment, I don't have to face my powerlessness over the fact that someday we may be separated—even if only for a short time—by death.

Therein lies fear's true and awesome power: It spawns many seemingly different concerns to keep us running around in circles and never facing the real source. We think we can stave off the thing we most fear by trying to block all the roads that lead to it. Yet anyone who lives with unresolved fear knows this doesn't work. (Though that doesn't seem to stop us.) Instead of preventing the outcome we dread, we create a host of smaller worries and convince ourselves we can control them. We can't, but we'll make ourselves frantic trying, and we'll do the same to those we love.

For example, a mother's greatest fear may be the loss of a beloved child. But instead of facing her powerlessness over that prospect, she concentrates on all the little attendant anxieties that she *can* control. She never allows her son to cross the street alone, skateboard, or make a friend of whom she does not approve. Or she becomes so busy controlling her daughter that she doesn't understand how she's already lost her to resentment, frustration and rebellion.

Most of us dread losing the person or persons we most love and depend upon. It is a terrifying and sometimes paralyzing thought. But we must acknowledge and confront this fear with faith if we are to avoid the many anxiety-based behaviors that damage us and our relationships—and stifle our trust in God.

The only power we have over what we fear is to admit we have *no* power. Seldom can we actually prevent the outcome that most frightens us, but the "dirt and gravel" we kick up trying will surely make a mess of things. That kind of desperate "circling of the wagons" serves only to trap us inside a very small circle and may cost us the very love we cherish. (Now *there's* something to worry about!)

Make no mistake about it: Admitting we are powerless won't feel good. Such an admission is no less than an acknowledgment that *only God* possesses the power we've coveted. This will be like stepping into an abyss we've scrupulously skirted all our lives. It will be dizzying. It may be terrifying. Certainly, it will be breathtaking!

Another way to describe it?

A leap of faith.

Prayer

Understanding Father, I've grown so attached to my fears. I've convinced myself that I can control outcomes by exercising a sufficient amount of worry and negative action. This false sense of power has comforted me in the past, though it may have hurt and alienated others. Help me to relinquish my need for control. Help me to trust you to catch me when I make my leap of faith.

Exercise

Think of an example of how you've hurt or alienated someone you care about by giving in to your fear and need for control. It could be a coworker you embarrassed because you were worried about looking good in front of your boss, a child you unwisely held back from some activity you judged too risky, a spouse you've nagged in order to relieve your own anxiety. Go to that person, explain why you did what you did, and apologize. Tell your former victim that you're striving to replace fear with faith and ask him or her to gently help you stay the course.

"I Leave You Peace"

With these words, Jesus provides the best possible evidence that God does not want us to be fearful or anxious: "Peace I leave with you; my peace I give to you." Yet for the chronically fearful, this message still hasn't sunk in. Jesus isn't saying, "Try to find peace," or "Try not to worry," or "Try to keep away fear and anxiety." He's not telling his listeners to rely on themselves for peace. He's not suggesting they somehow manufacture it. He's giving his own divinely generated peace to those who love him. He's making a gift of it, a gift that is offered to everyone. We just need the courage and wisdom to accept it.

Accepting this gift is the hard part. God's peace, which is essentially fearlessness, is not for the faint of heart. The divine peace offered by Jesus is the ultimate freedom from fear because it requires the absolute acknowledgment that *God* is in charge. *We can't achieve peace on our own!* We must accept it as it is offered, and that acceptance requires the admission that true peace can be grasped only if we are willing to remove ourselves emotionally and spiritually from the power of fear.

Few of us manage to achieve this level of peace, this utter absence of fear. It calls for the kind of faith that is all but impossible to human nature—the kind of faith that Jesus describes as able to move mountains, wither fig trees, and calm storm-tossed seas. This is the faith that affirms, "There is no point in worrying. God will take care of me. No matter what happens, God is in charge. I am not. Wherever I am, whatever happens to me, I will turn in trust to God."

While faith this unshakable may seem unattainable to those of us living with fear, we may take heart in knowing that every journey begins with one step. We can move, no matter how slowly, toward divine peace and complete faith. Before taking even that first step, we can gather courage by recalling again and again Jesus' words: "Peace I leave with you; my peace I give to you." Freedom from fear is what the Father, Son and Holy Spirit want for us. But before we can even begin to seek it, we must want it *ourselves*.

Elizabeth, an active young mother, thought she had done everything necessary to put herself on the path to divine peace...until she found herself immobile. She couldn't understand why she wasn't moving forward. She was, after all, doing all the right things: praying, meditating, sharing, reading scripture and inspirational literature. But her days remained as filled as ever with anxiety and worry. She found herself particularly obsessing over her skills as a parent, and as a result she began to stifle and overprotect her two young daughters.

"Finally," she recounts, "I realized I hadn't really started on the journey to faith. I had to go back to the beginning and ask myself some serious questions. The first was the hardest. Did I really want to attain the kind of peace, the kind of faith I professed to be seeking? Or was I still so tied to my fear that I unknowingly continued to reject the gift?"

Elizabeth began to understand that no amount of "faith work" would help if she weren't willing to open herself to God's gift of divine peace. She realized that opening herself in such a way would mean deliberately slipping the chain of worry and fear that kept her locked in old patterns. She also began to understand that if she herself were to be a good and nurturing parent, she would have to reexamine her image of God as a stern, heavy-handed Taskmaster.

She was learning that fear can become a dangerously comfortable habit. She started to compare fear to the old threadbare robe she'd kept for many years and continued to wrap around herself even though she had a closet full of newer clothes. She now says, "It took me a while, but I finally figured out that if I bought all the new clothes in the store, they wouldn't do me much good as long as I kept putting on the same old robe."

Prayer

Peaceful Jesus, I am often too little and petty to reach out for the peace you offer. Forgive me. Help me to do better, to stretch myself, to yearn toward your peace. Strengthen my heart and my resolve. Teach me to trust in you, regardless of how little I can trust in the world.

Exercise

Divine peace is not easily attained, but that doesn't mean you shouldn't try. Ask yourself whether you are willing to open yourself to God's gift of divine peace or are clinging to fearful patterns as if to a frayed old robe. Go to your closet or bureau and find an old, well-used piece of clothing that you should have gotten rid of long ago. Crumple it into a ball and throw it into a corner of your closet. Don't worry about whether it looks sloppy or slovenly. Leave it there. Consider it a symbol of your effort to leave behind old, negative, fearful ways. Every time you open your closet to select something to wear, look at that discarded item and let it be a reminder of your willingness to "put on" a new, deeper faith.

The Fine Line

When I started writing this book, I e-mailed an old friend to describe the project. It was late at night, so I was brief: "I'm writing a book about fear and anxiety."

The next day, her reply pulsed on the screen: "Wow. Great casting!"

I am the queen of fear. My friends know that if they can't sleep they can call in the middle of the night and pour out their worries. Not only will I be up, I'll be empathetic. There's probably nothing out there that I haven't worried about, and I've been waging my own battle against fear for nearly four decades. So, in the parlance of one friend, when it comes to anxiety, I "get it."

But even as I fight chronic, unresolved fear, I need to defend those many of us who are plagued by it. I need to say: Fear can serve a very important, even vital, purpose.

There. It's been said. And it is true. Anxiety about a health issue can lead a person to seek much needed medical help. Stories abound of spouses whose observant concern forces their partner to the doctor, there to find that the beloved is only a few hours away from heart failure or some other serious malady. Women worry about breast cancer, and as a result of that anxiety schedule the regular self-exams and mammograms that have saved many lives. A smoker who is tortured with anxiety about dying of lung cancer may finally quit. Fear of a house fire leads parents to drill their children on a safe escape plan, and when a fire breaks out all emerge safely. Anxiety about the superficial nature of a spiritual life can lead the lukewarm believer on a journey of deepening faith.

All these and many similar outcomes are good. And all are

motivated by fear.

The "sixty-four-million-dollar question" becomes where and when to draw the fine line that separates needless, dangerous, debilitating anxiety from useful, proactive concern. The stakes are high: One perspective is unhealthy and potentially devastating, the other is healthy and potentially lifesaving. The problem is that the two forms of fear can look so much alike.

When my mother worried about all the days I'd spent in the sun, I didn't pay attention. After all, I was olive skinned and dark haired. No problem. But to pacify what seemed to me to be her excessive worry, I visited a dermatologist. My cavalier attitude disappeared two weeks later when I saw the word *malignant* on the lab report from the mole he'd removed that very first day. Turned out, Mom's anxiety was of the healthy, lifesaving variety. On the other hand, I've since had to work very hard to keep from torturing myself over every new freckle or mole. Living with that kind of terror is unhealthy.

So how do we know the difference?

A very wise man, himself a cancer survivor, put it simply, "If you're worried about something you can impact or change with simple, direct action, then take the action and give the rest of your fear over to God. When you've done what you can do, stop worrying."

Sensible advice. However for most of us, taking it will require an action *and* an act of faith.

Prayer

Creator God, you made me. You know how breakable and easily damaged I am. Help me to be both faithful and sensible when it comes to caring for the precious body and spirit you've given me.

Exercise

Consider your list of worries. There is likely to be at least one (and probably more) that you can do nothing about. You cannot change it, effectively address it, or act to impact it. Go to a quiet place and clear your mind of this worry. You may not be entirely successful, but you should try. Accept that you can do nothing about your fear, that there is no sensible action you can take to diminish or eliminate it. Ask God to take over this fear now, since there is nothing you can do to address it in a positive way. After asking for help, make sure you deliberately release it to your loving Divine Parent. As often as your worry may surface in the next hours and days, that is how often you should remind yourself that you've given this particular worry to God. It no longer has a home with you.

Everyday Anxiety

Often it's not the big disaster that wearies us with worry. Daily life can be so fraught with routine anxieties and frustrations that we may find ourselves living in a web of worry without even realizing we've woven it.

There is a wonderful scene in the movie *What Women Want* that perfectly illustrates the prevalence of anxiety in today's world. Mel Gibson plays a character who finds himself stricken with the ability to hear the thoughts of every woman around him. After a day of "hearing" myriad anxious thoughts of women who range from a jogger who's having a furious conversation with herself about why her husband doesn't support her career to a waitress who wants a date with him but is terrified he'll hurt her, Gibson's character blurts out in astonishment to a colleague, "Women worry about *everything*!"

This is a stereotype, of course, for fear is no gender-specific curse. Arthur Miller recalled his reaction on the opening night of *Death of a Salesman*, his gut-wrenching play about the slow devastation of a career salesman whose life crumbles around him as he wallows in fear. Miller observed that there was a complete silence when the final curtain went down, and he was terrified the play had bombed. But when he looked out into the audience, just about every man was holding a handkerchief to his face. At that moment, Miller said, "I knew we'd struck a nerve."

Male or female, we all know the kind of nagging questions that can catch up with us. Why can't I stay within my budget? Will there be enough money when the kids reach college? Are my parents happy? If not, what am I supposed to do about it? Is it time to switch jobs, or can I stand this one a little longer? Why didn't I get the promotion? Will I ever find someone to

14

love and marry? Is my marriage as vital as it could be? Does my wife think so? Is my husband truly happy? Will our investments hold up so that we can retire someday? Is my daughter getting enough attention at the daycare center? Why can't my son get along with his teacher? Why is it taking so long to get pregnant? Can we afford a new furnace? Is that water in the cellar...again? What's that noise the car's making all of a sudden? Is that heartburn I'm feeling...or angina?

Or maybe just an ulcer from all this worrying?

It's scary how little fears can creep up on us. We started by fending off a few gently tossed snowballs and suddenly an avalanche is roaring down on us a mile a minute. Fear has a way of executing the kind of ambush that leaves us too vulnerable to fight back.

I'm not enamored of TV religion. I tend to avoid the nun who chastises her listeners with brutal sarcasm, and I'm even less thrilled by the three-piece-suited preachers who "sweat bullets" as they solicit donations between praises and hallelujahs. But I do enjoy one relatively peaceful program. It features spiritual music and short scripture passages superimposed over serene shots of nature. This program also has the occasional preacher, but he's usually dressed in jeans and more interested in soothing souls than counting sins and dollars. A recent segment focused on worry. "Do you know," asked the gentleman intently, "that statistics indicate that over seventy percent of the things we worry about never happen?"

I looked up from the book I was reading (with the television on as background noise). Suddenly, he had my full attention. It wasn't hard to translate his message into immediate practical application to my own life.

Seven out of ten of the things I'm worrying about *right now* will *never* happen! Or, more likely, even eight or nine!

It's easy for me to call up ten things that are nagging at me on any one day. But he had put a whole new twist on my daily burden: At least seven of those nagging things simply aren't going to happen. Regardless of how much time I spend on them—consciously and subconsciously; regardless of how they scratch up my stomach and clutter up my mind; regardless of how often I catch myself grinding my teeth over them...they are simply going to go away!

If I let them.

Prayer

Calming Father, you know how much time I waste on useless worry. You know how often my spiritual and physical health is impaired by so-called normal, everyday anxiety. Help me to relinquish this debilitating practice of habitual fear. Remind me that you provide the resources to meet the trials that do come my way, and help me to stop anticipating them.

Exercise

Sit down and make a list of ten things that are worrying you. Include everything that comes to mind, from how to keep your dog from chasing the mailman to whether your father will get into a nearby assisted living facility. Review your list, and then remind yourself that seven of those things will either take care of themselves or never happen. Then cross off seven items. Do not try to select the "least" of the worries; simply cross out the top or bottom seven regardless of how important they seem to you. You may not be able to immediately stop worrying about all seven issues, but post the list in a place where you'll see it often—the refrigerator door, a bulletin board, your mirror. Each time you pass the list, relax your body for a moment, unclench your jaw, take a deep breath, and remind yourself that habitual fear is a waste of time, health...and faith.

Godzilla

In the recent re-make of the classic monster movie *Godzilla,* the assorted scientists, military personnel, bureaucrats and government officials who are hunting the monster breathe a collective sigh of relief when they think they've finally exterminated it. But as they begin to happily dismantle their technology, weapons and makeshift headquarters in New York City, a renegade researcher makes a gruesome discovery: The creature has laid some eggs—quite a few eggs, it appears—and each is about to hatch its own man-crunching monster.

Fear is very much like the Mother-Godzilla. It can give birth to any number of ugly creatures. Some health professionals suggest that fear is literally the "root of all evil" when it comes to physical and mental well-being. And, as with the Mother-Godzilla, fear's creations are often as destructive as their parent...and sometimes more so. Uncurbed and unaddressed, fear can give rise to stress, hypertension, high blood pressure, migraines, back problems, heart disease, allergies, anxiety attacks, social disorders, ulcers, addictions, and a myriad of other physical and emotional maladies.

Fear can also be much more subtle, mutating into a variety of negative emotions, responses and traits. A husband who fears losing his wife may become jealous or overprotective, eventually acting out a self-fulfilling prophecy that might drive her away. A wife who is afraid to be alone may come to resent the time her husband spends on a hobby. When she expresses her resentment through sarcasm or disparaging comments, she will find herself spending even longer periods of time in separation and solitude.

A child who is frightened of school may make herself ill to avoid going, and this pattern may grow into a serious disease.

A teenager who fears being rejected by his peers may get involved in drug or alcohol abuse. A mother who worries unreasonably about her child may become overly strict and cause the very rebellion she dreads. A father who is obsessed with success at work may neglect his children and end up being a failure at home.

A woman who worries incessantly about wealth is likely to become more stingy and ungenerous with each newly acquired dollar or possession. An employee who is anxious about receiving a promotion may be so furious when someone else is promoted that his angry behavior could cost him the next promotion. A person who dreads social gatherings may withdraw and miss the opportunity to meet new friends.

All of us, in reaction to the threat of terrorism, can be filled with fear, anger, hatred, prejudice and a desire for vengeance.

The list of "fear spawn" is long and their negative impact is considerable. Fortunately, the grace of God is infinite and there for the taking.

Prayer

> *Dear Lord, help me to understand just how insidious my fear can be. Protect me from allowing my fear to create its own multitude of problems and issues. Give me the faith to completely eradicate from my life fear and its progeny.*

Exercise

Take an honest look at your fear. Examine whether fear has given birth to other negative issues and emotions in your life: anger? sarcasm? stinginess? reclusiveness? Make a list of all the undesirables that have been created by your fear. Go find a fairly large rock and then collect enough smaller pebbles to match the number of negative "fear spawn" you've identified in your life. On a counter, bureau or table, set the larger "fear rock" in the middle with the smaller pebbles around it. Starting the next day, focus on removing just one of the negatives from that day's experience. If fear has made you respond angrily to someone, try to leash your anger for at least that one day. When you've successfully completed a day without anger, you may remove one pebble from the table. Keep making the effort to remove one fear-borne negative from your life for one entire day. Do not remove a pebble until you've been successful for a twenty-four-hour period. It may take a long time before only the large original "fear rock" remains. Keep it there as a reminder of your commitment to keep fear from starting a "rock slide" in your life.

Be Not Afraid

Marion Bond West is an internationally known Christian writer. She is also a personal friend. We have corresponded for nearly two years now, faithfully, twice a month. I receive the same words that have inspired millions, except in a much more personal way.

Sometimes, I feel like ducking.

Marion lovingly pulls no punches. She is probably most well-known for her best-selling book *The Nevertheless Factor,* which describes how completely she surrendered to God to get through the most terrifying experience of her life—the loss of her young husband to cancer. The book advocates nothing less than utter capitulation, a willful acknowledgment that God is in charge and that trusting God is the only way to make it through life's crises...not to mention life itself. So Marion knows a thing or two about fear. She picked up on mine by the third letter.

"God does not want you to be afraid," she informed me in her responding letter, "but Satan *loves* your fear!"

Oh great! Now she's talking Satan. I don't even like to write the word, never mind consider the possibility. But Marion, in the best tradition of Christian evangelism, is all over the issue. She assures me that Satan can smell fear a million miles away. Why does Satan appreciate fear so much? Because it separates us from God. And Satan, Marion believes, enjoys nothing more than keeping us away from God.

Whether you believe in Satan or not, the idea that fear keeps us away from God simply makes sense. If we're consumed with anxiety and worry, how able are we to turn faithfully to God? If we're busy trying to prevent some outcome we dread, how likely are we to turn to God and say, "I know you'll get me through this no matter what"? And if Satan is literally the absence of God—as some theologians suggest—then giving in to fear does indeed put us in the realm of darkness.

So what does Marion do when she feels the kind of fear that brings Satan running?

"I pretend I'm not afraid. You see, Satan's too stupid to know that I'm pretending, so after a little while he'll just get bored and go away. (He's really not as smart as we think). And after I've pretended not to be afraid long enough to send him packing, I start to realize I really *don't* need to be afraid! It's all in God's hands."

Prayer

Beloved Lord, please help me to understand that when I give in to fear, I am giving away my trust and faith in you. I am embracing what is damaging and thrusting salvation away. It's so hard for me to push anxiety and worry away, but help me realize that when I do I make room for you. And I need you to be with me.

Exercise

Take a tip from Marion: Think of something that's worrying you right now. It can be something small or large, but it must be something that's nagging at you and keeping you from feeling and being your best. For at least the rest of today, pretend you are not worried about it. Even if you don't really believe yourself, act as if you do. Let those around you believe you are no longer anxious about this issue. Picture yourself thrusting it out of your mind and your life. Imagine the Holy Spirit coming to rest in the vacant space that had been occupied by this worry. Whether you imagine the Holy Spirit as a dove, as fire or as a divine figure, allow yourself to feel the calm of the divine presence. Breathe deeply and thank God for coming to your rescue.

The Still, Small Voice

Joseph Heller's book Catch-22 is based on the premise that people who act sane in this often incomprehensible, insane world are really the crazy ones, while those who appear insane are having the appropriate response to a crazy environment. The same premise might apply to fear: How can a sane person avoid fear and anxiety in this fearsome world?

A dose of the news—now available not just in the morning and evening but twenty-four hours a day—is enough to plunge any sane person into a frenzy of angst...if not pure despair. A sample of daily headlines and news leads reads like an introduction to the apocalypse:

- *Terrorists Attack America*
- *National Energy Shortage Reaches Crisis Proportions*
- *Armed Man Holds Daycare Center Hostage*
- *Study Investigates Link between Power Lines and Cancer*
- *Carcinogens Found in Drinking Water*
- *AIDS Ravages Africa*
- *Middle East Plunged into New Round of Violence*
- *Elderly and Infirm Often Abused in Nursing Homes*
- *Racial Violence Erupts in City*

The list goes on and on, each item more horrific and disturbing than the last. Some parents even censor their children's nightly news viewing the same way they limit violent television shows and video games. But how are parents and other adults to protect *themselves* from the devastating influence of today's world? How can those who pay even a modicum of attention to current events avoid anxiety? How are they to stay sane in what is, by much visible evidence, an insane environment?

"It's not easy!" admits Cathy, a self-described worrier. "Sometimes I feel so overwhelmed and distraught that I need to remove myself completely from the news reports. Of course, that's just a temporary solution, but it can ease the level of worry. I don't think we, as a society, realize how damaging it is to have this stuff coming at us constantly, all night and day. You hear a lot of people in my generation marveling at how our parents got through difficult times without panicking or even showing undue strain. Maybe the reason we have so much more difficulty today is that we're constantly confronted with all this negative stuff. We don't even get a chance to absorb it or figure it out ourselves before we need to explain it to our kids or shelter them from it."

Her sister Ellen, who claims everyone in their family has a "worry gene," agrees that it sometimes makes sense to "turn off and tune out," at least for a while. "Taking yourself out of the flow of continual news is not a permanent cure for anxiety, but it will certainly help," she says. "This kind of personal removal also gives you a chance to breathe, to process one thing at a time without trying to fend off the next hit. It keeps the worry flow at bay because it gives you the space to examine your anxiety in a more rational, quiet way. It helps you separate the threads so you're dealing with single strands and not one huge, scary knot of fear and despair."

Both sisters ultimately call upon faith to define their pragmatic actions.

"Quiet time alone won't make anything more than a dent in fear," asserts Cathy. "Even when the voice of sanity returns, you're still faced with what can be a very frightening world. That's when you really have to rely on God. That's when you need to listen only to 'the still, small voice.' Certainly, you should do whatever makes sense to address the issues at hand: I mean, if the newspaper says that the city water source is making people sick, don't use it! But, in the end, faith is the only real answer. You have to believe that God is with you, and you cannot destroy yourself trying to deal with every worry or impact every outcome. In fact, that kind of attitude is almost disrespectful to God. It's like saying, 'I'm not sure you can handle this, God, so I'm going to drive myself crazy trying! I trust you, God...but only sort of.'"

Ellen takes it a step further, asserting that faith can also be a source of guided action in a world that can sometimes seem faithless. She adds, "When I feel overwhelmed by the violence and cruelty that seems to engulf our world, I think about how Jesus lived, what he wanted us to do. That gives me new courage, knowing that I can *do* something. If I'm going to follow his teaching and his life, the best way to address my own fear and the world's anguish is to act with care and consideration, to simply be a decent, loving person to the people in my life today. It's not always as easy as it sounds, but if everyone did it, the news would never again be a horror show."

Prayer

Jesus, help me to stay sane in what often seems like an insane world. My loving Brother, help me to remember how you stayed focused on your mission of love and forgiveness even as your world crumbled into violence and cruelty. Teach me to replace my fear with action and my despair with kindness.

Exercise

When you wake up tomorrow morning, do not read the newspaper. Do not turn on the morning news. Do not look at the weather, the financial reports or even the talk shows. For the next twenty-four hours, shelter yourself from all news, regardless of its form or venue. Don't cheat by listening to an all-talk/all-news radio station in the car or checking your computer for a report of the day's events. Keep yourself completely insulated for one complete day. If you worry about missing something, take a deep breath and try to remember that God's in charge. God won't let you miss anything that will make you a better person, a more loving spouse, a kinder parent, a more empathetic coworker. Indeed, "missing" the news gives you the opportunity to work on all these aspects of your life. For these twenty-four hours, instead of worrying about the chaos around you, try to emulate the peace that was in Jesus. Make a conscious effort to treat everyone in your life today with focused kindness, respect and decency. If you succeed, you'll have made your *own* news!

Why Are *You* Complaining?

She was in her forties when she had her first stroke. As she puts it now, thirty years later, "The doctors thought it would come back, but it didn't." She doesn't mean another stroke, she means the use of half her body. Despite the years of physical therapy and medication, she never got back what the doctors had told her she might. For the past three decades, she's been partially paralyzed and has gone through life "making do" with the help of the unstinting love and generosity of her extraordinary husband. She has a lot of time to think...and a lot of really great stories. After an especially difficult period filled with new and old worries, she tells this one:

"I don't like to feel sorry for myself. I worry too much. I sit here and can end up worrying about everything. That's not good. We forget how many people have it more difficult than we do. Have you heard the story about the man and his cross? No? Well then.

"This man was plagued by all sorts of troubles and worries. He was burdened with money worries, family worries, health worries. He couldn't stop himself from worrying. He was afraid that God wasn't there for him. Finally, at his wit's end, he went to a priest. This priest was known to be a good counselor to people with big troubles who felt far from God. The distraught man poured out all his worries and fears to the priest. The priest was silent, watching him for a long time. Finally, the man cried, 'Father, what should I do? I can't live like this another minute!'

"The priest said, 'Go home and make a small cross using two slivers of wood. When you've made your cross, pray to God to

27

allow you to put all your troubles on the cross. Then do just that and bring the cross back here.'

"Pleased to be given something to do, the man hurried home and quickly fashioned the cross with two slivers of wood. But when he looked at it, it looked small and plain, even ugly. How could it hold all his troubles? Would the priest accept something so unremarkable and unattractive? He thought of adorning it with jewels or gold, but it was too small to hold anything more. Sighing, the man put it in his pocket and returned to the priest. Once he was brought into the priest's room, he took the tiny, undistinguished cross out of his pocket and showed it to the priest. He almost felt ashamed, and he was sure the priest was going to tell him to go back home and make a better cross. But the priest merely said, 'That is exactly right for you. Now, take it and put it in that room.' The priest pointed to a closed door leading to another room.

"Surprised, the man nonetheless did as he was told. Cautiously, he opened the door and walked into the room. He gasped in surprise. The room was full of crosses. A few were as small as his, but many more were larger. Some were huge. He realized that if all his worries could be put on his little cross, then many people must have much bigger problems than he did. His fears and troubles were nothing compared to some of theirs.

"'Father!' he exclaimed still staring at the room full of crosses, 'If God took away such overwhelming troubles from all these people, it should be easy for me to offer up mine!'

"There was no answer, and when the man turned around the priest was gone. Saying a deep prayer of thanks, the man left his cross in the room and returned home with a light heart."

Prayer

Lord Jesus, what is my puny cross compared to yours? And yet you carried yours so that I could lay mine down. Please help me to remember that when I feel overwhelmed by fear and far from you, I need only come to the foot of your cross and lay mine down.

Exercise

Make a small cross by gluing together two slivers of wood or small sticks. In a private room or alcove, light many candles. While holding your little cross in your hand, ask Jesus to give you the grace to transfer all your worries and fears onto the little cross. Understand that while you may feel your troubles are heavy, they will fit easily on this small cross. Pray for others who have greater burdens to lay on their crosses. When you've prayerfully transferred your worries to the cross, bring it to a place in your home where you keep a crucifix or rosary. Lay your little cross in the blessed space under or beside the crucifix or rosary. Whenever you pass by, use this tableau to remind yourself that you may always leave your fears at the foot of Jesus' cross.

Things to Do

Her husband was barely out of his middle years when they learned about his cancer. He'd led a rigorous life, making their living from the sea as a fisherman. Certainly he was away on the ocean more than she might have liked, but she'd understood that when they married. She'd accepted it, and he'd done well for them: property, a spacious home on the harbor with all the modern appliances she needed to raise their growing family. Over not so many years, he'd gained a reputation in the community for unsurpassing kindness and generosity. They had a sort of status. They were happy, settled.

That was all over.

He'd faced storms and waves, snow and wind, bruising hail and drenching rain—all the wrenching dangers of the sea—and had always come home to her and their four children.

Now he was gone, struck down by an enemy she had never known well enough to fear.

"But you must have loved him so much! *Needed* him so much!" I say to her.

She sits serenely on the couch almost directly under the arresting photo of him on his boat—wearing his cap, pipe clenched in his mouth, eyes scanning the sea. She smiles gently, these many decades later. "Loved him?" she repeats softly as if the comments are silly, but she's too polite to say so. "Oh yes. I loved him. Everybody loved him." Behind thick glasses, tears shine in her eyes. But her smile softens her tears.

"When he had to go out for days on the boat, didn't you worry?"

She chuckles, a sound no louder than a whisper really, and says, "Only during the hurricanes."

"When he died, what did you do? How did you cope?"

Not at all put off by the questions, she replies with one of her own: "What choice did I have?"

"But you had four kids! Your income was gone. You must have had so many things to worry about!"

She is quiet for a moment, as if considering all this for the first time. Then she tilts her head to the side and answers with great deliberation.

"I never really thought of it as having so many things to *worry* about. I guess I had too many things to *do*."

Prayer

Lord, help me to stop feeling sorry for myself when little things don't go my way. Teach me how small my fears and worries are compared with those of others. Let me become a doer, not a worrier.

Exercise

C hoose one of your most pressing fears and take clear, considered action toward resolving it. If you are worried that you and your spouse aren't making enough time for each other, schedule a quiet dinner together to talk about that. If you are worried about your many bills, make an appointment with a credit counselor. If you are worried that your emotional and physical health is suffering because you're not getting enough exercise, start taking a brisk walk every other day. You may not be able to completely resolve your worrisome issue with this single action, but you will have at least made a start. And more importantly, you will have *done* something, rather than wasted more time *worrying* about something.

The Best Medicine

"For days the refrigerator had been making strange noises," recalls Gretchen, a busy accountant, work-at-home mom and world-class worrier. "I kept saying to myself, 'This is the worst possible time for it to break down. It *can't* break down now!' I still hadn't been paid by all my tax season clients, and the refrigerator-freezer was packed with hundreds of dollars worth of food for a client reception I'd been planning. If the motor died, I'd lose all that to spoilage. Add that to the price of the kind of industrial-sized refrigerator-freezer we needed, and I just couldn't afford a breakdown now. I actually prayed for it to keep chugging along!

"I became like the kitchen police. I rationed the number of times the kids could open and close the refrigerator and freezer doors, practically shrieking at them if they dared open the door just to browse. Whenever they did go into the freezer compartment, under my close and mean scrutiny, I made sure they firmly pressed the door closed. I would even give the door an extra push myself to make sure it was tightly shut. I somehow thought that would keep the motor from having to work too hard. I guarded and coddled that appliance as if it were a newborn!

"Then the day before the party, a massive thunderstorm came roaring through and cut off power for twenty-four hours. I lost everything, of course. After all my worrying and vigilance, nature defeated me! While the kids gleefully sucked up the melting ice cream with straws, I put my head down on the kitchen table, not knowing whether I was going to laugh or cry. I ended up settling for a sick grin when I remembered something my mother used to say in situations like this: 'God got me!'"

Gretchen's mom didn't really believe that God sends minor disasters to teach us lessons, but the prospect of ironic humor is indeed inherent in excessive worrying. We worriers can't help noticing these laugh-or-cry events, and it can certainly seem that God is pulling us up short. When Gretchen told her mom the whole tale, the mother replied, "Well, honey, that's what we get for worrying!"

The lessons for Gretchen were fairly straightforward. Worrying is a waste of time and effort, a waste of life. In fact, worrying can be a laughable enterprise. In Gretchen's case, though, the lessons went deeper. For a parent, they always do.

"When the power finally did come back on, the refrigerator was working perfectly!" she relates, smiling ruefully. "No noise, no breakdown. At that point I really was ready to laugh. But then, a couple of days after the party, my youngest was in the kitchen. She was very quiet and still. That in itself was unusual, and I figured I'd better investigate. When I went in the kitchen, she was leaning against the refrigerator with all her tiny weight, her palms pressed against the door. Her little face, contorted with determination, brightened as soon as she saw me. 'Look, Mommy,' she piped up, 'I'm helping keep the 'frigerator fixed.' All of a sudden, the situation wasn't quite so funny. You know, the last thing I want to do is pass my anxiety on to my kids. I hadn't thought much about how my behavior was affecting them. I still can't get her scrunched up little face out of my mind."

Laughter may indeed be the best medicine for anxiety. It may also be the lesson-cure from on high.

Prayer

Joyful Lord, thank you for the many chances you give me to laugh at myself and my fears. Thank you for showing me the irony of groundless worry. Help me to learn from these opportunities and to recognize when my fear is no laughing matter to those I love.

Exercise

Right now you probably have a frivolous worry. You may be fretting about something that may never happen or, if it does, really won't be that important in the long run. But you've let this small thing take on larger-than-life proportions. Your obsession may even be affecting others. Imagine yourself sitting down across from God for a little talk. Tell your Divine Parent all about this thing and ask for help in seeing how silly, how truly small, it is compared with the important matters in life. Then, laugh with God. That's right, laugh: at your fear, at yourself, at the fact that you're laughing with God! Start with a smile, then a chuckle, then a couple of forced laughs. If you're lucky, you'll soon be laughing at the absurdity of it all.

The Prayer Warrior

For most of his life, my friend Norman hasn't exactly been what my mentor, Marion Bond West, would call a "prayer warrior." He knows I pray, and he certainly knows I pray for him. But until relatively recently, his own prayer life has been, well, let's just say somewhat restrained.

That seems to be changing. I'd like to think it's my influence, but it's God's! Norm has started praying more. At first he'd just join me halfheartedly in a quick blessing or thanks offering. After a while, he actually started sounding like he meant it. Even more recently, he'd bring some of his own suggestions to the table. To his credit, he's not a fearful person, so his prayer is never borne of anxiety as it is with so many of us worriers. A few weeks ago, he taught *me* something about prayer...and about fear.

Norm called one afternoon and without even bothering with a "hello" exclaimed, "On the way to work this morning, I pulled over to the side of the road and prayed!"

I almost dropped the phone. Norm's usually a madman on the way to work, always trying to pass the slow drivers and beat his best commuting time—with cell-phone in one hand, coffee in the other. That is not what I would consider an ideal prayer setting. Particularly not for him.

He continued: "I got a call that a meeting had been cancelled because a colleague had been rushed to the hospital. No details, just that it was serious. I don't even know the woman that well, but all of a sudden I felt tears in my eyes. Without even thinking, I pulled over to the side of the road. Some guy I'd passed twenty miles back blared his horn when he flew by, but I didn't even care. I just closed my eyes and prayed for this woman and her family. Just a quick, quiet prayer like the ones you say. When I opened my eyes and started the car, I realized that I actually believed in it! I actually believed in prayer...*my* prayer.

"I'd always had this sort of cynical perspective of prayer, like 'hey, what about all the people who don't get what they need or pray for?' But during the rest of the drive to work, I started thinking about all the prayers that *do* get answered—little and big things that people pray for every day. When those prayers get answered—and they do, every single day—there's no fanfare. The cynics don't talk about all the prayers that get answered—just the ones that don't seem to be answered. Look at you! Look at how many of your prayers are answered every day, and you just take it in stride. You pray every day that I travel safely and return home safely, and every day for years I have. You pray for your writing to be guided by God and well received, and it has been. You pray for health and the grace to deal with whatever comes, and you've been given both health and the grace to deal with the not-so-healthy times. You pray for healing, and you've been healed.

"And I thought to myself, if so many prayers get answered every single day all over the world, there's got to be something to it. It's got to be worth doing."

I hung up the phone with Norm's amazed joy still ringing in my ears. And my ears were ringing on their own a little, because as a wise older friend says, "If your ears are ringing you must be ashamed of something!" I *was* a little ashamed. It seemed that without trying especially hard, my friend Norm had quickly surpassed me in both the sincerity and the faith of his prayers. He'd stopped dead in the middle of his frantic day to offer a prayer for a near stranger. And then he'd rejoiced in the efficacy of that prayer. He hadn't worried about whether it would work. He hadn't called the office back to see if his colleague was recovering. He didn't worry at all about the details, and he didn't let fear about the outcome overrun him.

I, on the other hand, have specific routine prayer times. Spontaneity does not play a big role in my life or in my prayer life. The very idea of pulling over on a busy street to pray makes me nervous. I almost always pray most fervently for things I want or need for myself or my beloveds. I save my more sedate prayers for others, almost as if I want to make sure God understands my priorities. And my prayers are almost always accompanied by worries: What if God doesn't do *this*? What if *that* happens despite my constant prayers? I am ashamed to admit that I pray in contingencies. And it is all too seldom that I step back and offer God thanks for the myriad blessings and answered prayers I receive every single day.

I could start by thanking God for my wonderful, extraordinary friend Norman, the prayer warrior.

Prayer

Lord, sometimes you surprise me with a mirror. But I'm not always proud of what I see. Please help me realize that I can change and that you provide me the catalyst and the courage to do so every single day.

Exercise

Surprise yourself with prayer today. At some point in the day, you will be presented with the opportunity to offer a brief heartfelt prayer that you might not ordinarily make. It may be hearing about a coworker who is sick or going through some trouble. It may be seeing a homeless person or someone begging. It may be a natural disaster in this or another country. It may be something as simple as being passed by an ambulance or hearing sirens. If you've found no opportunity by the end of the day, simply watch the evening news. Something will surely present itself there. Keep your heart open, waiting for this opportunity. When it comes, stop everything you're doing and offer your prayer. It should be sincere and trusting. Do not wonder if your prayer will be answered. Have no doubt or fear. When you're finished, be sure to offer God thanks for all blessings and all grace.

Sweating the Small Stuff

Right after Christmas, a friend called in an absolute dither. A newlywed, she'd just returned from the first "Officially Married" holiday at her in-laws. Her mother-in-law, by all accounts a relatively benign woman, had made the seemingly naive remark that my friend very much resembled her husband's first wife.

"In front of everyone!" my friend squeaked in outrage. "His whole family was there, people we hadn't even seen since the wedding, and his mother's telling them all that I look like his ex-wife! And all I could think was that all these people were sitting at our wedding and watching me and thinking, 'Hmmm, not much different from last time, except for the dress.' And my husband didn't say a word! Didn't deny it, didn't even give his mother a look. I couldn't believe it. I felt like crawling under the table, and I haven't stopped thinking about it since."

There was a long pause. Then she asked in a much lower voice, "*Do* I look like her?"

I said something I hope was soothing, but the fact is that I know my friend very well. If it weren't this, it would be something else. If during Christmas dinner her mother-in-law had trilled, "Well, I've never seen two women who are so utterly different as you and Johnny's ex," my friend would still have had an anxiety attack. And she'd still be fretting over the innocent comment, wondering if her husband had been attracted to her only because she was so completely different from his first wife and not for her own specific attributes.

My friend is an expert when it comes to "sweating the small stuff." So much so that in her life small stuff doesn't stay small for very long. Any number of well-known adages could be used to admonish her. For example, there are what some antistress advocates have dubbed the two most important rules of life: "Don't sweat the small stuff," and "Everything is small stuff." Then there's the more old-fashioned version that every mother has said at least once: "Stop making a mountain out of a molehill."

But for those of us plagued by fear, these rather cavalier instructions are easier given than carried out. I don't believe for one second that my friend enjoys the great anxiety in which she regular immerses herself. Sometimes she even feels foolish, acknowledging that she's "borrowing trouble." She once admitted, "My favorite part of the New Testament is where Jesus tells his disciples not to worry about food or clothes or wealth or beauty because God will take care of all that, and besides, they can't change anything anyway! And he tells them not to worry about the future because 'Today's troubles are enough for today.'

"You know, I really believe all that. I have faith that his words are true. I read those passages over and over again. I just wish I could *live* them!"

After nearly causing a fight with her husband over "the Christmas incident," as she's come to refer to it, my friend decided she needed to take at least a small step toward living her faith. Realizing that she wouldn't stop "sweating the small stuff" all in one day, she began slowly by signing up for yoga and tai chi at her local YWCA. She is finding that the deliberate, studied movements and positions help slow down her mind and relax her body. "I hadn't realized how often my body was tensed up, in attack mode. It was as if I were constantly on the defensive, even from a physical perspective."

That's not at all hard to understand. It takes a lot of energy to build "mountains out of molehills."

Prayer

Dear Lord, help me to stop focusing on the little worries and irritations of life. Reveal to me how often I create big problems from small issues. Teach me to live my trust in you rather than just talking about it.

Exercise

If the eyes are the window to the soul, the face is the mirror of the soul's stress. Tics, jaw grinding, rigid cheek bones, "face" headaches, rapid blinking, watering eyes, ringing ears, and frown lines are all telltale signs of worry and fear. If you "sweat the small stuff," you may regularly experience any or a number of these stress symptoms. Sometimes treating the symptoms can be the first step to treating the disease. If you feel unable to tackle your whole anxiety problem at once, start with your face. Spend ten or fifteen minutes every morning sitting in a quiet, relaxing place. Music is acceptable as long as it's soft and unintrusive (music will actually help if your ears are ringing). If you are up early enough, you may light a candle to help dispel the darkness and set a gentle mood. Do any or all of the following simple exercises, focusing on where stress wreaks the most havoc on your face: Unclench your jaw and move it around in a circular motion. Close your eyes and keep them still so they are not darting around behind your eyelids. Loosen your tongue from where it may be pressing against the top or bottom of your mouth. Gently roll your head around on your neck, but do not try to force through any pain you might feel. Be conscious of whether or not you are frowning. If you are, relax the grimace. Finish by placing a cool or warm (depending upon your preference) washcloth over your face for a few minutes. If stress builds up as you proceed through your day, remember to take a few seconds to renew these practices.

Faith vs. Freud

M s. Claire has been a children's librarian for over a decade. She has observed more than a few anxious children in her time, not to mention many anxious parents. Anyone watching in the children's rooms will see kids of all ages make a beeline for her as soon as she comes into their line of vision. Even the smallest ones cry out and wave their chubby little hands at her from their parents' arms. She knows everyone by name and seems to calm the fears of old and young just by her presence. So what has she learned about fear from all this experience, including her increasingly successful efforts to conquer her own anxieties?

"Fear is all about ego," she states matter-of-factly. "It is the ego that gets in the way, separating us from God. The ego brings on fear whenever we start to move in a new, joyful, more trusting direction. The ego hates it when we finally learn to depend on God and not on ourselves. As soon as someone starts to give themselves over to faith, the ego will rebel against it. That's why so many people have a hard time concentrating on prayer or yoga or any spiritual exercise that will bring them closer to God. The ego is fighting against their success."

Ms. Claire has watched enough young egos-in-the-making to know whereof she speaks. The ego wants what it wants and wants it now, much like the average child (and the average adult, for that matter). That's precisely what she's suggesting: Children—and adults—are most comfortable relying on themselves. We need only to watch a child struggle for independence to see how basic is this need for self-reliance. As if on cue, Ms. Claire points to a little girl who is vehemently refusing her mother's efforts to select a picture book for her. She is determined to do it herself. And yet adults, at least, know that no one can truly rely only on himself or herself. Life's disasters and tragedies prove that soon enough. But as Ms. Claire points out, the ego rejects any attempt to relinquish self-reliance and turn completely to God. The ego, therefore, will chose fear over faith any day.

However, she says, life can still be a journey toward God, a quest for faith, a search for miracles. Not surprisingly, this librarian conducts her search through words and images. She is a strong advocate for journaling and does it every day herself, but she warns, "You have to keep writing beyond just the chattering and diary-type stuff. If you want to address your fears, you need to keep writing until you can bring them out in some way, identify them and, hopefully, start to resolve them."

She also looks to less traditional methods when it comes to developing faith and banishing fear. She believes that miracles are discernible in everything, and she's constantly on the lookout for them. She makes it a practice to select books—for herself as well as library visitors—that address spirituality in creative and interesting ways. She also likes to find movies that offer the prospect of a moral or faith lesson, explaining, "I find myself watching specifically for how the character and the writing portrays—or doesn't portray—faith. I'm interested in seeing how a character either gives in to the ego and fear or manages to clear away these impediments to faith."

She will soon retire as the children's librarian. But creativity and her search for faith will take her on a journey that may include leading book discussion groups, visiting Mexico, writing, pottery, "and whatever comes next." One thing's for sure: She'll face the future with her fear carefully in check.

Prayer

Lord, open me to your grace. Help me not to allow my ego to separate me from you. Please let me discern the many lessons, both creative and pragmatic, you offer me each day.

Exercise

G o to the movies with your spouse, family or friend. Or bring a movie home for the VCR or DVD player. Spend time selecting a movie that will offer a spiritual, moral or faith theme, though it need not be a "religious" movie. However, many of those will work fine. Some more recent religious productions include the made-for-TV movie, *Jesus*, as well as *Romero, Joseph of Nazareth, Jesus Christ Superstar, Godspell,* and *David.* Movies that are not religious depictions can also carry strong spiritual, moral or faith messages. Disney offers a host of animated movies chock full of history and morality. Other screenings could include *Pay It Forward, The Green Mile, The Messenger, Kolya, Mr. Smith Goes to Washington, Guess Who's Coming to Dinner, Ordinary People, The Apostle, Mississippi Burning, The Diary of Anne Frank, The Life of Miss Jane Pittman, Brother Sun/Sister Moon, The Color Purple, Schindler's List, Remember the Titans, To Kill a Mockingbird, Gandhi* and *Forrest Gump.* These are just a few possibilities. Keep in mind that many of these titles are not appropriate for children (even some of the traditional or religious movies depict horrific violence) and choose accordingly. Plan to have dinner or a snack after the movie and spend time discussing it. Give people time to explain how the movie affected them. Discuss how different characters did or did not express fear or show faith. Talk about whether the movie will change your lives or perspectives in any way.

Do Something Scary

My favorite photograph of my father is one in which I can barely see him. Certainly I wouldn't be able to recognize him if I didn't know who it was. It is a long-distance shot; he is far away, posed on some rocks that jut way out into the ocean. It might be Cape Cod or the coast of Maine. He is wearing a sweatshirt with the hood up. The waves and sky look stormy, gray. He is facing the ocean.

His arms are raised in the air, as if he's challenging the storm. No, it's as if he's triumphed over the storm.

If you knew my father, you'd know why it might be hard to recognize him in this photo. He is not one to take undue or unnecessary risks. When my sister and I were kids, he would clutch our hands in his every time we went anyplace he considered even remotely dangerous. While other kids were climbing over slippery rocks or cliffs, we were well behind the safety rails, my father gripping each of us firmly. At seaside resorts, we walked several yards away from the edge of the boardwalk, peering around my dad to catch a glimpse of the water. Before stepping upon any department store escalator, we were carefully inspected for any loose or dragging clothing that might get caught in the stair feed. By the time he considered us old enough to use the huge slide at the hotel pool where we stayed for a week every summer in Cape Cod, we were too embarrassed to clamber up the ladder with the little kids.

Dad was into safety. And worry.

That's why I was so surprised when he told me he was considering early retirement. Sure, I knew that after over thirty-five years with the same company, he deserved a break. No one I knew deserved a break more than he did. And sure, I knew that work had become increasingly unrewarding and tense for him. No one I knew worked as hard or as diligently as he did. And yes, I absolutely wanted him to retire and start to enjoy life.

But the idea of my father considering early retirement? My father, who'd worked every day of his life since he was fifteen years old? My father, who never purchased anything—anything—on credit? My father, who tracked pension plans, IRA interest rates, insurance benefits, cost of living indices like a starving hunter looking for dinner? My father, who did his own taxes year after year because he was determined to understand the process? My father, who never borrowed anything from anyone in his whole life? My father, who worried whether my mother and he would have the quality of life they wanted in their retirement years? My father, who had saved up for our college and weddings...before we even entered high school?

I watched while Dad went through the agonizing process of confronting and resolving every concern and fear he had regarding early retirement. He did all the legwork himself, studying costs, making plans, examining accounts. He painstakingly looked into benefits, pension payments, stock options. He carefully considered what he might like to do after retirement...besides play golf.

I don't think I have ever been as proud of anyone as I was of my father on the day he took early retirement. And shortly after he made and implemented the hardest decision of his life, that picture of him triumphant on the rocks was taken.

Sometimes the only way around fear is through it.

Prayer

Lord, help me to understand that some risks might well be opportunities you've sent me. Let me also see this kind of risk as an opportunity to truly demonstrate my faith.

Exercise

Do something scary. Take a calculated risk. Today, instead of trying to skirt around one of your fears, take a deep breath and walk right through it. You may select the fear—and the risk you'll take—ahead of time, or you may wait until a particular worry rises up to meet you. To remind yourself of your commitment to walk through fear today, wear tennis, walking or running shoes all day long. If your job precludes such footwear, wear the most comfortable pair of shoes you own. Every time you look down in dejection, fear or cowardice, take good note of your shoes. Today, you are meant to take a risk and run right through it. Lift up your eyes and plunge through the fear!

Parental Surrender

I don't for one minute imagine that it was easy for my parents to, well, be parents. It's not easy for anyone to be a parent, and there is no role more fraught with the potential for anxiety. Over and over again, parents claim that the worrying starts from the moment they take their infant home until...forever. Jobs change, money comes and goes, sickness and health weave in and out of a life, even death comes knocking only once, but parenthood is a full-time, life-time proposition.

It also seems this may be the toughest time to be a parent. Never mind the usual worries of money, normal safety, sickness, school performance and costs, adolescence, dating and marriage. Those are minor league anxieties for today's parents, who must consider terrorist attacks, violence in schools, a culture of peer pressure and bullying, rampant drug and alcohol abuse, sexuality issues, eating disorders, and intense competition in just about every aspect of the child's life. Even today's most easygoing parent is probably losing some sleep.

So, how do parents do it? How do they decide what to worry about and what to let go? How do they address issues like guns and knives and gangs in school? What do they say when the latest incidence of international violence is blared all over the nightly news? How do they know when their own fears threaten to create a fearful child rather than simply a safe one? How do they give their children a sense of faith in a world that can seem faithless and even hopeless? How do they even let their child leave the house in the morning?

"It's not easy," declares Jaye, who is determined that her beautiful little daughter's vast enthusiasm for life not be stifled. For Jaye and her husband, it's all about balance. But that's not always easy to achieve. Her intense belief in God as the Spirit who lovingly imprints all creation helps.

"I want our daughter to get a sense of the goodness in life, the Spirit of God in and all around us and everything," explains Jaye. But that doesn't stop her from worrying about all the day-to-day issues—from how to explain the death of a beloved pet to which school is the better choice for their child. In the end, Jaye says, it comes down to faith...and a certain degree of surrender.

"I don't think you can raise a child today unless you have faith," she affirms. "I was just saying to my husband, 'If kindergarten is this hard, how are we ever going to get through adolescence?' But, I come back to two things. First, fear is taught, and I don't want to teach our daughter fear. The second thing is the most important aspect of being a parent, and that is to know that God loves her even more than we do. After all, how could we even let this little person go out the door every day if we didn't believe that God loves her more than we do?"

Prayer

Vigilant Father, help me to remember that you are always with me and those I love. You, Father, are the ultimate, loving Parent, and in your presence fear has no place.

Exercise

It is unrealistic to expect that any parent can be completely worry free. It may even seem impossible to surrender your child's welfare to God. Ultimately, however, God is there for your child when you can't be; God is there for your child *al-*

ways. It may help to practice the belief that God is the ultimate Parent—indeed, the Parent of every child and of every parent. If you have children at home, take a moment after you see them off to school, daycare, or other activities to thank their Divine Parent for loving them and remaining with them when you must be absent. If your child is no longer at home, offer the same prayer after you next speak or write to him or her. Ask our loving God to also help you with your fears for your children. Let yourself accept the glorious truth that the Parent who watches over you and your children loves you all more than you can love yourselves.

Spilling Over

She was a worrier. He was not. But they'd been together for many years, and he had learned, somehow, to accommodate her fears. He tried to help her stay calm. She tried not to let her anxieties control their life together. Sometimes she succeeded. More often, she did not.

It wasn't her gut-wrenching fears that most often caused them trouble. He could understand, even if he didn't share, her "biggies": serious illness, death, accidents, harm coming to their children. But it was the small, day-to-day stuff that got him down.

"I've always had a hard time simply enjoying things," she explains. "Little—and even big—bits of good news would get swallowed up in my tendency to worry. One of the kids would come home with an A on her report card, and my next sentence after, 'Good work, I'm proud of you,' would be 'I hope you can keep it up, and you're not disappointed with the next report card.' My sister, a breast cancer survivor, would call to report a clean bill of health from her latest physical, and my first impulse would be to wonder if the doctor had missed something. A collector would call to say he wanted to purchase one of my paintings and, right after thanking him, I'd say to myself, 'Right, I'll believe it when I see the check!'

"Everything with an upside had a downside of new anxieties for me. But what was worse was that all my stuff was spilling over onto the people I loved. I was building my own personal wall of shame, and I didn't even know it."

This woman didn't think too much about how her constant worrying affected her family and particularly her husband. She just expected everyone to recognize and accept her worrying ways. She didn't let herself realize how she was eroding the simple pleasures and anticipations of their lives—or her own.

"Then one day, my husband woke me up late on a Saturday morning. I'd been painting late into the night, and he'd let me sleep in while he went downtown to pick up some groceries. He had the most joyous look on his face. He told me that he'd seen the arts editor of our state's largest daily newspaper at the store. The man was going to run an article on my latest show— a very complimentary article, according to my husband who was beside himself with pride and delight. Barely noticing the look of pleased anticipation on his face, I tumbled back into bed and grumbled, 'Oh great. Who knows what he actually wrote? What if he does me more harm with buyers than good?'

"I carried on in that way for some time before I bothered to look over at my husband. His face was utterly crestfallen. He looked as if I'd just slapped him. Without another word, he got up and left the room.

"All of a sudden I felt sick to my stomach. A gaping chasm opened inside me. I ached for him. *What had I been thinking of?* What was I always thinking of? I had girded myself for life like it was a constant battle, and I expected my husband to be fighting at my side. But sometimes when I wielded my fear like a defensive weapon, he was the one being wounded."

Later that day, she told her husband how wrong she'd been to react so negatively, so anxiously. She told him she was sure the article would be wonderful, a boost to her career. But the excitement had fled for him. She'd driven it away, as she had so many times in the past.

Now there was only one thing left to ask herself: "Do I want to keep doing this?"

Prayer

Father, you give me so many reasons, small and large, to rejoice in the course of my life. Help me to embrace these exciting moments and events. Teach me to avoid turning good news into bad with my fears. And let the lesson not be too costly.

Exercise

Do you have a wall of shame? Can you think of times when you've spoiled or diminished good news by fearing there would be bad news to come? Have you disappointed someone you love by responding to exciting news with worry instead of joy? Consider these transgressions against those you say you love. Ask yourself if you want to continue to be a dimming force in the lives of your family and friends. If the answer is *no*, vow to make a proactive change. The next time someone approaches you with exciting news, take a deep breath and force yourself to rejoice with them. It won't be easy, and it won't be your initial reaction. But you can ignore the old familiar voices in your head that immediately start to clamor about complications and problems to come. And if you can't ignore them, push them aside. Refuse to give them a voice. Instead, congratulate. Express pleasure. Act thrilled. Share delight. And in the face of the person who trusted you with joy, you will find your reward.

Solitary Containment

She immediately knew the answer to her own question. She didn't want to continue this way, diminishing herself and damaging her husband and loved ones. But she also knew that she had ahead of her, as her mother used to say, "a long row to hoe." Yes, she had faith, but she also had years and years of negative, anxious thoughts and behavior to overcome. She believed her faith would prevail, but she was wise enough to know that complete victory would not come by merely hoping for it. She began to ask herself how she could take practical action to support and strengthen her faith.

Admittedly, she was working against a lifetime of fear. Her first reaction to anything, invariably, was to worry, to look for the "bad" side, to anticipate a problem. "I knew I wouldn't be able to change fifty years in one day—or one week or even one year!" she says. "I had to accept that it might take another half-century to completely turn this around. In the meantime I wanted to employ 'containment' strategies that would help me live my faith and improve my marriage and other relationships. I didn't want to keep hurting and disappointing the people I loved the most."

She asked God to guide her efforts...and then she began to walk. And bike. And perform yoga ("I'm not always calm enough to achieve the mental stillness, but I *can* do the physical movements"). Sometimes she would just take time to think or listen to music. After a while, she would deliberately use this time to face whatever fears were plaguing her. She did not try to drive them away or ignore them. Indeed, her plan was quite the opposite. She gave them center stage.

"Not only did I let the fear run free during these hours, I started playing out the same anxiety-laden encounters with my husband and family and friends that I'd always had. Except now, I did it all with conversations taking place only in my mind. If I was worried about my son flying to Chicago for a job interview when a February storm was predicted, for example, I would complain to at him in his absence (during my solitary containment time). 'I don't see why you have to go at this time of year,' I'd tersely tell him in my mind 'What if you get stuck there and miss work at your real job? Why can't you wait for better weather? Is it that important? Is it really worth risking your life?'

"I didn't answer for him—or for anyone whom I brought into these imaginative encounters. Instead, I just let myself go with both barrels until the sharpest stabs of anxiety began to fade. Sometimes my mind would naturally wander onto other thoughts or simply become quiet. I found that my need to actually carry out these conversations in reality lessened drastically. If was as if God's peace flowed into the space that had been vacated by all that poisonous anxiety.

"Gradually, something really astonishing—and wonderful—started to happen during these silent sessions. I'd find myself ranting on about whatever was worrying me to whomever was involved, when suddenly another voice would intrude. The first time it happened I was chastising my husband in my mind that if he *really* cared about what *I* wanted, he wouldn't even *consider* this new position that meant even more time away from home. As I doggedly worked through this scene, the voice came: *'How can you possibly doubt that he cares about you and what you want? Think of the many ways he defers to you: buying your home, making investments, planning vacations. Surely you don't really believe this devoted, thoughtful man doesn't love you or care about your needs.'*

"I began to hear this voice more and more often in a variety of imagined encounters. I knew it wasn't mine; I'm not that rational. It was God whispering in my mind's ear, helping me along on my journey to fearless faith."

Prayer

God of all journeys, please lead me. I don't know how to change, only that I must. Help me find my way to you and, in so doing, to more loving and unselfish relationships.

Exercise

Try to find time every day to decompress. Fear is a great energy sapper. It will debilitate you and diminish your ability to think clearly and make good decisions. If not every day, at least three times a week, set aside time for yourself to exercise. Use that time to carry on your own solitary, silent conversations. Express your worries and anxieties as you move and stretch your body. Don't hold back the way you might if the person were present. Gesture, rant and rave if you feel really pressured by fear. Let these scenes play out until you can let them go or until you become a little weary of them, but try not repeat them in "real life." Let these imaginary encounters remain between you and God. And remember to listen for the Lord's voice: that quiet, reasonable, gentle whisper that might just join in.

He Bore Our Infirmities

He had no form or majesty that we should look at him, nothing in his appearance that we should desire him. He was despised and rejected by others; a man of suffering and acquainted with infirmity; and as one from whom others hide their faces he was despised, and we held him of no account. Surely he has borne our infirmities and carried our diseases; yet we accounted him stricken, struck down by God, and afflicted. But he was wounded for our transgressions, crushed for our iniquities; upon him was the punishment that made us whole, and by his bruises we are healed.... And the Lord has laid on him the iniquity of us all.

The above is not the description of some beggar or homeless person or drug addict. It is not the description of a Holocaust victim or the target of terrorism in the Middle East. It is not the description of someone dying of AIDS or Alzheimer's or cancer. It is not the description of someone who is starving or the victim of domestic abuse.

Though it might be all of those.

It is Isaiah's prophetic description of what Jesus, as man, would suffer. Christians share a common belief that Jesus suffered so brutally for our sins, for the sins of humankind from the beginning of time, to effect forgiveness and salvation. But Jesus' suffering had more than that divine, blessed purpose. His suffering had an entirely human element and purpose as well. He suffered so that whenever we are afraid we can turn to him. We have our model in him, and just as importantly, we know that *he* knows exactly how we feel.

He knows exactly how pain feels. He knows exactly how humiliation feels. He knows exactly how rejection feels. He knows exactly how exhaustion feels. He knows exactly how frustration feels. He knows exactly how grief feels. He knows exactly how sorrow feels. He knows exactly how it feels to be cut, stabbed, beaten, stripped, mocked, slapped, hated, scapegoated, blamed, scorned, disgraced, starved and suffocated.

As *Daily Guideposts* editor Andrew Attaway puts it, "No matter what we are going through, no matter how sick or sorrowful we feel, we can always look to the cross, because hanging there is the One who went through it for us, and before us, and who rose after it was all over. That is our ultimate comfort."

Jesus paid an extraordinary and terrible price so we could be comforted in the normal travails of the human condition. Knowing that is the starting point of faith and the beginning of overcoming fear.

Prayer

Jesus, I sometimes forget how you suffered. Or maybe I just can't bear to think about it. The physical pain you endured would be intolerable for anyone else. As I confront health issues, help me to remember both how horribly you suffered and how utterly you—and thus all of us—were healed on that blessed third day.

Exercise

Read the prophecies of Isaiah about Jesus and how he would suffer and be rejected (especially chapter 53). As you read these scripture passages, stop at each description and think about someone you know who fits Isaiah's words. Think of someone who has been reviled, perhaps a neighbor whom no one cares for. Think of someone who has borne your infirmities, perhaps a parent or partner who has cared for you in illness. Think of someone who has been spit upon, perhaps a homeless person or panhandler you've seen. Think of someone who's been beaten, perhaps the child or wife of someone you suspect to be abusive. Think of someone who has been rejected because of illness, perhaps someone suffering from an addiction or AIDS. Now consider that Jesus, our ill and suffering Lord, is in each of these people. Pray for each of those people, even those you don't know well at all. Remember that Jesus suffered, died and rose for each of them as well as for you.

Healing Fear

"If you've got your health, you've got everything." "I don't care whether it's a girl or a boy, as long as it's healthy." "Money can't buy you health."

These familiar adages demonstrate the great importance of good health. Of course, that's probably why it is the issue that causes more worry, anxiety and terror than almost any other. Money can be lost...and made. Love can be lost...and found. Relationships can be hurt...and healed. But health is perceived as a precious commodity that once taken away may never be fully restored. After all, the endgame of poor health is death. And even when people survive serious illness, they are seen as being somehow permanently wounded, as if they will always be vulnerable to poor health.

Of course, with today's technological and medical advances, these perceptions are no longer true—but that doesn't necessarily mean they've changed. "My generation never even uttered the word *cancer*," acknowledges one mother in her sixties who is trying to cope with her son's diagnosis of cancer. "We called it 'the Big C' or 'the C-word,' as if not saying it would protect us from it. To us, the mere diagnosis of cancer seemed like a death sentence, and even though I know that many, many people survive and go on to live full lives I still have a hard time even saying the actual word!"

She's not alone. But as this woman struggles to be a loving, supportive mother, others don't even want to be associated with someone who is fighting serious illness. One home-based business writer tells how she did not disclose her heart disease to all of her editors and clients. "I told the ones I knew would understand—the ones I knew had some personal experience with sickness," she says, "but I didn't tell those I didn't know well or particularly trust. I was afraid I'd stop getting assignments." Later, when word got around, she did indeed lose an important client. She remains convinced it was because he'd learned about her disease.

When we avoid sick people (and we do), it isn't because we are cruel. It is because we are afraid. The dread of illness can be consuming. My friend Elizabeth reports, smiling, "My dad was so afraid of germs that he wouldn't even come into the room when my brother or I had a virus. It was almost comical. My mom was always the one who did the "dirty work." We knew it wasn't that Dad didn't love us, but we realized he was terrified of getting sick, missing work—all that. He would stand in our doorway and kind of wave at us, smiling sheepishly."

Elizabeth has two daughters of her own now, and she thinks she now understands better her father's attitude. "Becoming a parent has definitely made me a more understanding daughter. I know now that having young children can be like incubating germs," she laughs. "Whatever they pick up in school or on the playground comes directly home. And usually, they have a bug for twenty-four hours, and then they're up and at it. When my husband or I get it, however, we're down for the count for several days. These viruses usually hit the adults hardest."

That's why Elizabeth has more empathy for her father. She knows now how helpless a sick adult can feel, and she does indeed worry about staying healthy. "When my husband or I catch a virus, we might miss work or be unable to care for the kids—especially if they're still recovering. The logistic problems alone can be staggering. Talk about feeling vulnerable! And sometimes I worry, 'What if one of us gets *really* sick? How would we manage? What if it's him? How would I manage without his help, his love, his strength, his support?' If I think about it too much, I can get really worked up. And I definitely understand how Dad felt."

Most adults can identify with Elizabeth's worries and feelings of vulnerability. People in the "sandwich" generation— who are concerned about both their children *and* their parents—can feel particularly burdened. How do we keep from feeling completely overwhelmed by the dread associated with illness—either our own or that of someone we love? How do we conquer the fear of being unable to cope?

A very wise woman who has spent many years counseling and caring for the sick and the disadvantaged, Sister Mary Louise, has an extraordinarily simple and beautiful answer. "I believe in *actual grace*," she writes. "It is grace to help you get through something, grace to help you *act*, to be able to act."

It is the grace that allows us to overcome our fear.

Prayer

Father who gives all grace, when it comes to illness I feel grace-less because I am so afraid—for myself, for my spouse, for my children, for my parents, for my dearest friends. I'm afraid I won't measure up if illness puts me down. Help me, Father, to remember about actual grace. And when the time comes, help me open myself to receive it.

Exercise

Think of someone you know who is sick: a parent, a child, a friend, perhaps even a neighbor or someone from your church community. Say a prayer, asking God to open the person's heart and mind to actual grace. Then perform an act of grace by calling or visiting the person yourself. Put aside whatever fears you may have about whether or not it's "catching" or whether your visit may be too depressing or upsetting. Pray that God opens you to actual grace. When you visit, listen closely to the person. Let him speak his fears. Let her talk of her memories. Ask him if there's anything he needs. Touch her. Hug him good-bye. Sometime soon, return for another visit.

Stacking the Deck

It's hard for a sick person to let go of fear. Sadly, the health care process can make that nearly impossible. For those who've felt trapped in the health system, it can seem the most frustrating, unnegotiable, confusing and downright debilitating labyrinth they've ever experienced.

A friend living with cancer speaks in a voice so exhausted that it's barely discernible. She describes the hours she spent one day on the phone with the insurance company, the doctor's office, the pharmacy and the hospital. "And that was just to get bills straightened out," she says wearily. "All that wasted time had nothing to do with being treated or healed. There are so few days when I can work or even take a walk. It seems a shame I had to spend the afternoon like this."

Others echo her great frustration. They tell of insurers who refuse to pay, sky-high costs, the troublesome process of getting referrals, botched tests, mixed-up lab reports, incompetent technicians and uncommunicative doctors. Even those not inclined to fearfulness often find themselves besieged by countless worries as they try to negotiate the medical maze. Some tell horror stories that make it easy to understand why people who are already sick, frightened and weak despair of getting the care they need.

My friend with cancer says they shouldn't. Though she's fallen into just about every possible ditch on the road to wellness, she believes that people who are ill must stand up for themselves because, as she puts it, "It's a matter of faith. I feel this way about it: In the midst of everything I'm going through, I deeply believe that God loves me. I believe he's created me as his own and, therefore, I have value. I *am* valuable. So when I feel it would be easier to just give up, I take my strength from that faith. I am too beloved by God to let myself get lost in this process." Acting for herself on the basis of that faith has taught her a great deal. She offers advice for those who feel confused and even terrified by the health care system:

- Be proactive. Don't wait for someone to do something for you. Know what your insurance policy does and does not cover; don't wait for the doctor or the pharmacy or the hospital to tell you. Arm yourself with information.
- Ask questions. The doctor or the lab technician or the nurse may seem formidable or rushed for time, but you must insist on getting the answers you need. You can be courteous *and* insistent if you need to be.
- Give information. The fact that you have an unusual ache or pain may not seem important in the greater scheme of what you're going through, but it could provide the medical professional with a vital clue. Fill out all surveys completely, and refer to them when you talk to the doctor, technician or nurse so that you can confirm they've read your file. The more they know, the better able they are to treat you.
- Knock the chip of your shoulder. It does no good whatsoever to project an attitude of distrust and hostility. Granted, the health care process can be a trying one, but you should project a positive attitude, a sense that you expect to get excellent treatment. You should also make an effort to treat with respect and courtesy those treating you. Mistakes may be made, but you needn't assume them from the outset. You can be assertive without being someone everyone in the office dreads.
- Follow-up. This is hard. The last thing you'll feel like doing some days is to call the lab or the insurance company or the doctor's office, but it is vital to your physical health and emotional well-being. Don't be a pest—if you know the test results won't be in until Tuesday, then don't start calling on Monday. But you do have the right to seek information that will help you make decisions. You also have the right to seek closure on worrisome financial and medical issues. A calm mind is the best healer.

Finally, my friend counsels, "Don't make yourself miserable. If you need to take some time off to rest from the rigors of pursuing wellness, by all means do so. Take a vacation. Give yourself a break. But never give up. You must persist in seeing that you get the best care on earth...because you've got the best care in heaven!"

Prayer

> *Healing Father, I get so tired and discouraged*
> *trying to deal with my fear. I'm so confused by all*
> *the problems and options associated with health*
> *care. When I feel like giving up, remind me that I*
> *am your beloved child. Show me that my life is*
> *valuable to you and that I deserve to have others*
> *treat me accordingly. Lift my spirit, Father.*

Exercise

Was there a time when you were worried or upset by the health care process? Have you ever returned home from a doctor's appointment or a medical test and berated yourself for not asking the right questions or insisting on the attention you needed? Have you ever felt let down or, worse, betrayed by the health care system? Sit or lie in a quiet place and send your mind back to that time. Picture yourself back in the doctor's office or the lab or on the phone with your insurance company. Now change the tape. Replay the scene with you taking a proactive, assertive role. Say what you should have said. Ask what you should have asked. Conduct yourself with the dignity, self-respect and courtesy worthy of God's child. Promise yourself to keep this scene—and your faith—in mind the next time you face a similar situation. When you finish rewriting the scene in your mind, sit down and write a letter to the health care professional, lab or insurer in question. Detail your concerns or disappointment. You may either mail the letter or not, but keep in mind that mailing it might aid other patients.

A Most Vicious Cycle

There are few things worse than being sick. Unless it's being sick and worried...or worried sick. It is the cruelest of cuts, then, that the two seem to go hand in hand. For some, ill health and fear are so inextricably linked that it is difficult to determine which came first...or whether one might be causing the other.

Such a causal relationship is almost always in effect with illness. Medical science has documented the significant role stress plays in exacerbating and sometimes even causing illness. The equation is simple and proven: fear = stress = disease (literally "*dis*-ease"). But this linear formula takes on a more sinister aspect when it becomes circular. The link between worry and sickness provides the perfect example of a vicious cycle: the more we worry, the worse the sickness; and the worse the sickness, the more we worry.

Inserting faith into this cycle of fear and disease is a way to slow the pace of both. People coping with serious illness report that taking a faith action—such as attending a healing service, practicing centering prayer, participating in a retreat, or simply praying more—can give them a vital sense of calm and even control.

"I can't say I really had a close relationship to God before I developed AIDS," confesses a young professional who works in the insurance industry. "My life was all about my career and enjoying what little free time I had. I was terrified when I found out...not just for my life but also for my job. What if someone at the company found out? What would happen to my job future? Did I even *have* a future to worry about anyway? How much time would the drugs give me? Were they as good as people had been saying? This stuff was rushing around my head so much that I couldn't even be sure if I was feeling bad from the virus or bad from fear. I was calling in sick already because I was so debilitated and confused. I could hardly function.

"Then my sister invited me to a prayer service at the church she attends. I thought she was nuts, frankly. I couldn't even face my job or my friends, but I was supposed to drag myself out on a Friday night to church? But she insisted, even came to pick me up, and at that point I figured I didn't have much to lose. If nothing else, I'd be spending some time with her, and that was something we hadn't done for a while. We'd grown up going to church, but I hadn't been for years. In fact, I was sort of surprised that any church even offered an AIDS healing service.

"It was an amazing experience. It wasn't so much that the service was earthshaking or that my guardian angel came down and sat on my shoulder the way we'd been taught to think as kids. It was just a quiet, gentle Mass. No judgment, no expectations. The church wasn't packed, but there were people alone and grouped together—portions of families like my sister and me. I think it was the quiet that got to me more than anything. I realized that nothing had been just silent since the time when the doctor told me. There had been no peace, no calm, no *quiet*. I didn't realize how important that could be. All the clamor in my head just stopped.

"Hey, who knows, maybe my guardian angel *did* come and sit on my shoulder!

"One thing for sure, my sister and I have become closer—real confidantes—like we used to be as kids. I don't know how the virus will progress, but I know I'm coping with it much better now."

For people struggling with disease and fear, taking time out for an act of faith can be a lifesaver—literally and spiritually.

Prayer

Jesus, Lord, I know I make illness worse with worry. My fear only intensifies the pain and exhaustion, and I become more confused. Help me to seek the quiet and calm that is available to me only in your presence. Let me step out of the vicious circle and into your peace.

Exercise

The next time you experience fear associated with being unwell—whether it's because of a migraine, a virus, an injury, an inexplicable pain, or something more serious—force yourself to step out of the vicious cycle. Set aside time—daily if possible—to practice faith. Choose something that is most in keeping with your own style and personality. Your practice can be informal and solitary, such as meditation on God's mercy, prayer, scripture reading; or it may be part of a more structured process, such as a regular healing service, faith support group, retreat or inspirational reading group. Put aside any skepticism you may have and try to open yourself to the experience. Promise yourself you will clear out the fear for just this short time. Allow that newly vacated space to be filled with silence, calm and a sense of community with the Holy Spirit, with family, with friends.

Open to God's Respite

If anyone must rely on faith even more than the person who is worried and sick, it's perhaps the person who is worried and the caretaker of someone who is sick. Not only is the caretaker carrying around her own fear about whether she'll be able to fulfill this demanding role, she's weighed down with the many details of care. Add on her very real fear for her sick loved one, and the combined burden becomes all but unbearable. Without respite, the caretaker may herself become ill.

There are people, agencies and programs who can provide physical respite, but spiritual respite will make the critical—and lasting—difference. There are no easy answers here, no clean-swept paths. A determined will to faith is the only possible solution. For someone exhausted with worry and care, this requires no less than an opening of the heart and mind and soul to God: an admission by the caretaker that she can do only so much, anticipate only so many needs, spend only so many hours and days wrangling with insurance companies and doctors, and offer only so much comfort and relief from pain. It is an admission, simply, that she is not God, and that despite all her attempts to control and fix and heal, she may ultimately fail. And finally, it is an admission that even if that happens God will not fail.

Caretakers who make this leap of faith often acknowledge being surprised by the sense of relief they feel. Those who were raised in a faith tradition say that the essence of their religious upbringing comes flooding back into their lives. They experience it as a force that is often stronger than the superficial religious habits and beliefs they've picked up along the way; it is much more than just "window dressing."

"I'd gotten away from the church as I grew older, so the possibility that I could receive any sort of comfort from faith did not seem real," reports Sue, who cared for her infirm mother until the mother died. "But I had a friend who'd become a priest, and he suggested I attend an evening retreat for caretakers at his church. Different people spoke about their experiences, and even though I didn't say anything, I felt tears filling my eyes. I hadn't ever given myself the chance to cry. I'd never wanted to show that to Mother. Then the Sister who led the group advised us to let go of our fear and bitterness for just these two hours—to accept God's respite for just this little while.

"I felt like something in me was cracking open. At first I thought it was just the exhaustion sweeping me away. That's what I told myself—that it was lack of sleep and maybe even hysteria. But it wasn't. My eyes were closed and I literally saw myself breaking open. My body, my brain, my heart. A fissure opened and all the worry, the fear, the weariness I'd been carrying around in me came pouring out. I felt almost weightless! Then there was all this light and warmth pouring into me. I knew it was from God. I just knew it! And I knew that I would have to keep myself broken open like this if I wanted to continue to experience such healing."

Sue's vision is very like what other caretakers have reported as they reached out toward God. Those who've been separated from their faith—or those who admit to a faith life that was no more than going through the motions—report feeling particularly shaken by their "opening" experiences. The challenge, as Sue acknowledges, is to leave the self and the soul open to this life-changing faith. "My inclination was to shut myself down again as soon as I went home to Mother," she confesses. "It just seemed that all my worry and fear couldn't coexist with this new openness...and that's just the point. Fear and anguish cannot live for long in the warmth and light of faith."

Sue is quick to caution caretakers that faith and strength won't be evident every single moment. There will be times of darkness and great weariness. But the caretakers who are "opened" will never completely lose touch with that abiding faith. And they will go forward, knowing always that they have access to God's respite.

Prayer

Gracious Parent, let me open myself to your respite. Help me to "rest in you" and to know that your rest drives out fear and refreshes eternally. Give me the courage and the energy to return again and again—as often as I need—to your comforting embrace.

Exercise

Focus on a current situation in which you are a worried caretaker. It may be a traditional role wherein you are caring for an ill friend or family member. Or you may be "taking care" of a troubling issue in your life, such as a job change or a wayward child. Arrange for physical respite, or space, from your caretaking burden. Depending upon your personal style, you might chose to join one or two understanding friends for a couple of hours, or simply go off to a favorite place on your own. Close your eyes. Breathe deeply. Allow your weariness to wash over you. Give in to it. Imagine yourself opening to God. Feel God draw out all your frustration and fear. Let yourself be cleansed of all worry. Keep yourself open and feel divine light and warmth pouring into you. When you return to your caretaking, hold the image of your openness in your mind. Whenever you need it during the upcoming week, draw upon this spiritual respite—this gift of God.

Love ≠ Worry

I grew up believing that if you really loved a person you really worried about him or her. Period. Simply put, love equaled worry, and if your worrying disturbed or even derailed the beloved, so be it. If you worried about others so much that they didn't do something they really wanted to do—like joining the Peace Corps, for example—well, that's all part of love, right? You had only their best interest at heart.

As I grew into young adulthood, I probably understood (rationally, at least) that there was something wrong with this picture. After all, I was a proud member of the Oprah Generation. I knew what was what in terms of personal growth and evolving relationships. But emotionally and spiritually, I clung to my first model: Worry equals love; end of story.

And it might have been the end of my story were it not for two things: cancer and my husband. Less than a year after being diagnosed, I met the man who would become my husband. It took months for me to tell Charlie that I had a cancer diagnosis in my recent past. Some women keep old lovers or bad credit histories secret. Not me. My deep, dark secret was cancer. I kept that secret for much longer than I should have. And the longer I waited, the more I feared that someone else would tell him.

My anxious inner debate was endless. How could I tell him? Would he feel obligated? Of course he would. He was the kindest man I'd ever met. And then how would I be able to tell obligation from real love? How would he? Would he turn and run? If I gave it more time, would he react better? Would I seem pathetic to him? Would worrying about the future be too much for him?

I decided to wait. Then came the weekend exactly one year

from my initial diagnosis. I'd had two melanomas removed and, since they were in the initial stage, completely eradicated. Subsequent biopsies had been negative. But I would still need to go for six-month skin checkups, watch for changes myself, and endure a number of biopsies as my doctor literally pared away areas of my body that looked a little suspicious. It hadn't occurred to me that this first anniversary would have any undue effect on me. After all, it wasn't exactly something to celebrate, was it? But I found myself edgy and near tears the whole weekend.

Over that weekend, it rained and rained and rained. Then it got foggy. Then it rained some more. Late on Sunday, this wonderful man turned to me and said, "You know that—now and for the rest of our lives—we should always talk. There is nothing either one of us could say that could drive the other one away. You can tell me anything, anytime." With that, I burst into tears and blurted out the nasty little secret like a blubbering child.

Charlie's eyes never wavered. He held me until I finished what must have been an overlong explanation filled with details he didn't need at that moment. Then he asked when my next biopsy was scheduled. Studiously, he retrieved his calendar and wrote in the appointment...in ink. Given the intensity with which Charlie works, the love he has for his work, and the hours he puts into it, this should have told me all I needed to know. The idea that he would plan something two months ahead of time that would take him away from work should have been enough.

Still over the next days I watched anxiously for signs of either flight or repressive duty: the deer-in-the-headlights look, the hangdog look, the pitying look, the eye-rolling look, the brow-furrowed-with-worry look. I saw nothing remotely resembling any of these. In fact, it was as if I'd said nothing at all! My fear gradually dissolved into something that felt suspiciously like annoyance. By the next weekend, I had only one question for him: "Doesn't it worry you?"

"What?" He looked at me blankly.

"That I've had cancer!" I all but shrieked. He blinked once

and then gazed at me steadily for a while. Finally, in the same level voice with which he'd questioned me the weekend before, he said, "No, I don't worry about it. I try not to think about it too much. How could I, and go on? I have faith it's gone. But I'll be with you, no matter what, through every biopsy and anything else. If we have to fight it, we'll fight it. But worrying won't help me prepare for any of that. And besides, I've got your next appointment in my book."

For the first time in my life it struck me in my core (and not just in my brain) that worrying really doesn't have much to do with loving. Or anything else useful, for that matter.

Prayer

Clear-sighted God, thank you for showing me the difference between loving people deeply and being always afraid for them or afraid of losing them. Help me to keep these separated in my life and my relationships. Help me to remember that love always builds up, while fear always tears down.

Exercise

Have you convinced yourself that worrying about others is the same as loving them? If you have, it's time to face the truth. Obsessive worry can only hold back and discourage your beloved, whereas active love will support and strengthen them. Think of someone you love and worry about constantly. Now take that worry and turn it into a loving act. If you're worried about your spouse's upcoming medical appointment or test, schedule time to accompany him or her. If you fear your child is doing poorly in school, make an appointment to see the teacher so you can work together to find the problem. If you're afraid your friend is clinically depressed, check into therapists in your area and urge him or her to make an appointment and offer to drive. If you worry that your elderly parents aren't eating well, go grocery shopping with them and help them choose lots of prepared meals that they can heat up themselves. Then sit with them while they eat the first one. Your life is brimming with opportunities to turn worry into love. Pick one and do it!

Imaging the Divine

Sleep is often the first casualty of fear. Anyone who has spent a long night wrestling with a troubling problem knows this. The fact that anxious sleeplessness is an extremely disturbing experience is evidenced by the myriad sleep potions and prescriptions advertised on television—especially at night! The commercials usually feature a man or woman who looks about ready to shriek with frustration and tension. The person paces, sighs, gestures aimlessly, tosses and turns in bed. The night is dark. The clock radio gleams cruelly. Sometimes it even ticks, just to make sure the message gets across.

Then, one tiny pill later, everything is bliss. Our once sleepless hero is snuggled up under the covers as the moon peeks in a window. The face is peaceful, the limbs relaxed. Clearly the dream is a good one. And of course, the inevitable voice-over assures the audience that the pill, potion or prescription is not habit forming or at all dangerous. No side effects. No problems. Except, of course, it shouldn't be taken for more than a week or two and persistent sleeplessness should be addressed by a doctor. And, oh, anyone with liver problems or diabetes shouldn't even be in the same room with this pill....

Insomnia, difficulty falling asleep, inability to get back to sleep—these can all be manifestations of worry, anxiety or fear. And no pill will chase those away—at least not permanently.

Ellen, who hails from a family of worriers, has spent more dark hours tossing and turning than she wants to count. She's tried everything: reading in bed, *not* reading in bed, staying as motionless as possible, getting up and roaming around the house, watching television, listening to the radio, finishing house or work projects. She even purchased different tapes: one of white noise and, when that failed spectacularly, one of whales peacefully "singing" at sea. Same result.

"I thought maybe praying would work, but it didn't," she says and adds laughing, "or, I should say, I didn't pray in a way that worked. I'd start hounding God to let me go to sleep, to solve whatever was worrying me, to fix everything. After a little of that kind of so-called praying, I was more wide-awake and nervous than before! I'd be wondering what I was doing wrong that God would put me through all this. Was I being punished? Was there something wrong with me? It really got depressing. And then, of course, the more exhausted I became, the less able I was to fight off the anxiety and resolve anything. Some days when I finally did crawl out of bed I couldn't even decide what to wear to work.

"I'd tried so many 'sleep techniques' that when someone at work—who had probably made note of my bedraggled appearance and purple-circled eyes—suggested what she called 'prayer imaging,' I didn't know what to think. I didn't want to offend her, so I just listened. She described a kind of silent prayer—praying that didn't involve words at all. She said it was a matter of letting loving images of God come into your mind and that most people have specific images that comfort them. These God-images come from their childhood or from pictures or words in books they've read, and many include themselves in the images. The important thing, she said, was not to try to pray frantically with words but to focus on loving God-images and offer those as our prayer.

"She gave me some examples of what had worked for her, but I was still skeptical. On the other hand, I'd tried just about everything else, so it seemed foolish not to try this. At first, it was hard. I was so accustomed to praying a certain way...with what my husband calls my polite 'hostage list' of demands: 'God, please do this, and I'll be a better person; God, please do that, and I'll stop being so frantic.' So, it was difficult for me to just lie down silently and let a wordless image of God come into my mind. Then I remembered what she'd said about including myself in the image. Somehow that made it more real for me. I started imagining myself as a little child running and running across a field toward God. And when I reached him, he picked me up and swung me around in the air. I could see myself laughing and laughing. I even let myself feel the sensation of being swung around in the air. Sometimes I could actually feel my face relaxing into a small smile as I lay there in bed.

"But the image I've come to rely on the most is one I use on the nights when I'm most desperately worried or down about something. In this one, I picture God sitting on a bench on a cliff overlooking the ocean. It's nighttime, the waves are pounding below, and a cold wind is blowing. I'm wandering around on the cliff, freezing, lost, alone and frightened. Then I see God, just sitting there and waiting for me. I stumble over to him, too scared and weak and tired to even run. He lifts me into his lap and wraps me in a blanket. He holds me against his chest and I feel the soft, soft cloth of his robe. I close my eyes. The wind still blows, but now it feels warm. The waves still pound, but now they lull me to sleep. There are cuts and scrapes on my feet and legs, but now they are healing. I just lie there, feeling his power and love. I know it is for me.

"I can't say these images always put me to sleep. But they do give me rest."

Prayer

Wakeful Father, you need never sleep. I do. Help me to remember that you are always keeping watch over me and that no fear can stand under your scrutiny. Help me to sleep peacefully in your vigilant love.

Exercise

The next time you have trouble sleeping because you are worried, arrange yourself in the most comfortable position you can manage and close your eyes. All the lights should be off. There should be no blaring television or radio. Breathe deeply for several moments. Try to calm your mind. Let the darkness envelope you. Now envision God holding you as if you were a small child, rocking you slightly, comforting you. God knows that you are troubled and need peace. You need not catalog your worries; God already knows them. Relax, knowing that you can stay in the divine presence as long as you wish. If you don't drop off to sleep, simply rest in God, keeping your mind and body still and focused on a particular prayer image.

What If...Faith?

Irene, a gentle and brilliant therapist, helped people deal with all sorts of fear-related problems. She knew better than most how fear can cripple a life. People came to her with job stresses, fractured families, tense marriages, and a host of other life-strangling issues. Most of their problems, if not all, were based in fear. Irene understood that a person doesn't have to be suffering anxiety attacks every day to feel under attack by anxiety.

She had a blunt tactic to help her patients face down their fears. "What if?" she would ask. And then when the patient stared back blankly at her, she would explain, "What if the thing you're most afraid of actually happened?" Often, just getting the person to respond was a challenge. Most fearful people spend a great deal of energy trying to avoid examining dreaded outcomes, and the idea of driving fear to its ultimate end can seem even more frightening.

But Irene would insist. She knew that most fears become huge because no one ever reduces them to an appropriate size. She also knew that she could not diminish fear for her patients. It wouldn't help in the long run if she provided the answers. The patients needed to be led to do it themselves. Only then would the power of fear be dissipated.

Her patients learned a great deal about themselves in this process, occasionally even discovering that what they most feared might actually be an opportunity. One woman who went through Irene's "What if?" process recalls, "I started seeing her because I was having trouble speaking up at work. I'd been with the same company for almost twenty years, and all of a sudden they were hiring new people from the outside, without rewarding or promoting internally. I could have accepted it if the new people were more qualified, but that was not the case. More often, the old-timers like me would end up training the new younger employees, and then we'd watch them be promoted over us! It really started to get to me. Originally, I went to her to see if she could help me speak up. After I told her all this, the first thing she did was to ask me what I was *really* afraid of.

"It's funny, though, I didn't even have to think. I just blurted out, 'I'm afraid I'll lose my job if I speak up!' She just looked at me and asked, 'And what if that happened? Then what?'

"Well, frankly, that was the one scenario that I'd been trying to avoid, so I'd never thought about what I'd do if it happened. Losing my job was what I didn't want to happen. But she gently insisted I continue. I had to think about it for a minute. At first I was terrified. What *would* I do if I lost my job for speaking out? But then I started thinking: I'm not happy there anyway. That was a big surprise to me, to realize I really was not happy at work anymore and knew deep down inside that they weren't going to change their policies, whether I spoke up or not. The more I talked with her about it, the more I realized that the best outcome for me would be the one I'd thought I was most afraid of.

"Except now, I would do it on my own. I wouldn't waste my energy getting myself fired. Instead, I could take my time and have another job lined up before I gave notice. I could do it at my own pace. From there, we talked about job-change strategies and how I could determine what I really wanted to do. Making myself answer the question 'What if?' was really quite an eye-opener for me. I was still afraid, but I wasn't paralyzed. I have to admit I was even a little excited!"

Although many people will discover that their greatest fears are not that great at all, not everyone who asks "What if?" will find their life immediately changing for the better. It can take work to transform the dreaded outcome into something positive or simply manageable. In some cases, outcomes will still seem frightening, though not nearly as frightening as when they are allowed to fester unexamined. That's where faith comes in. Faith takes Irene's challenge "across the finish line."

Prayer

Father, sometimes I let my fear take on massive proportions. When I fail to confront it, my fear runs rampant. Give me the courage to face my fears and the faith to know that my future is safely in your hands.

Exercise

On a blank piece of paper, write down one of your fears. Just below this, write the question, "What if it happens?" Then answer it. Include all possible outcomes. Follow them through to their logical ends. Keep writing until you feel you've weakened the power and reduced the dimensions of your fear. When you've finished, hold the paper in your hand and offer a brief prayer to God. Then take the paper and lock it in a drawer. If and when your fear returns, retrieve the paper, re-read it, add any more "what ifs" you can think of, and then put it back under lock and key. Place the key by a statue or symbol that gives you strength.

Antidotes to Fear

Seeing the word *malignant* on a lab report with your name at the top of the page has a way of escalating the process of establishing priorities. This can be a surprisingly positive development in the life of a worrier. The physical and spiritual journey of surviving the disease can bring many blessings. For example, aging doesn't seem like such a bad deal after all!

Approaching middle age, some women worry about wrinkles, investigate skin creams and hair dye, fret over diets, fear they may lose their "youth," nervously consider estrogen therapy and anxiously implement workout regimens. I, on the other hand, found myself thrilled to greet each passing year. On my thirty-seventh birthday, I was wrestling with a diagnosis of cancer, and as a result my *fortieth* birthday was really something to celebrate.

Most women my age hope to "age gracefully." I hope to age, period.

But I wouldn't mind doing it gracefully. To help me with that, I've looked to people who have indeed aged gracefully and, in the process, confronted their fears. Actually, it seems that confronting fear and developing faith are integral parts of successful, dignified aging. And as I've been fortunate enough to discover at a relatively young age, anxiety about aging is a small thing compared to the fears some of my most graceful models have confronted.

I think of Sara and her husband Richard, now in their seventies, who thirty years ago together faced the fact of Sara's crippling stroke. Faith faltered for a while but then came roaring back as they took up the fight to lead dignified lives within the bounds of a most loving marriage. They've dealt with their many health-related fears and questions by becoming extremely well-informed on medical issues and breakthroughs. Information, for them, is power. Today, they still guard each other's hearts and memories with astonishing ferocity. Any afternoon you can find them in their cozy living room—Richard blowing out Louis Armstrong jazz classics on his trumpet, Sara sitting at her desk working on household bills and correspondence.

Now that's dignity.

Mary has been a widow for three decades, having lost her husband to a painful battle with cancer. Alone for the first time in her life, she wasted little time on brooding or bemoaning her fate. She became an active and very welcome support to her four children, her grandchildren and, later, her great-grandchildren. She visited with friends, kept a garden and even mowed her own lawn. Though she now lives with sight and hearing impairment and diabetes, she has few complaints. "After I turned eighty, things *did* go downhill a little," she says in her quiet, matter-of-fact voice. "I'm lucky. I can still cook and do whatever I want to do in my house." When a new neighbor from across the street walks over to say hello, Mary explains cheerfully, "Now, don't mind me if I don't notice when you wave. It's just that I can't see you. I'm not being unfriendly or anything like that."

Now that's grace.

Then there's the order of women religious who've cooperated with medical scientists in a long term study of Alzheimer's disease. The results have stunned and delighted the medical community, not to mention given great hope to the rest of us. It seems these Sisters, who belong to an active community, are helping scientists prove that lifestyle can have an important impact on the disease. The Sisters, who are described as being very involved in their communities and ministries while also engaging in exercise and intellectually stimulating pursuits, demonstrate a faithful, positive outlook. Many of them live well into their eighties without showing any symptoms of Alzheimer's, even when autopsy results later indicate that the disease had taken hold. According to one of the Sisters, their strongest shared attribute is a good sense of humor. Of the medical study, she quips, "When we die, our souls are going to heaven...and our brains are going to a lab in Kentucky."

Now that's faith.

Dignity, Grace, Faith: antidotes to fear.

Prayer

Lord of all time, help me to be grateful for every year—every minute—you give me. Instead of worrying about aging, let me grow in grace, dignity and faith with every new year.

Exercise

Take a piece of paper and draw a line down the middle. At the top of the right side, describe your most graceful characteristic. At the top of the left side, describe your least graceful characteristic. Under your most graceful characteristic, make a list of six actions you can take to strengthen and enhance this characteristic. Under your least graceful characteristic, make a list of six actions you can take to weaken or eliminate this characteristic. Starting with the six actions you can take to weaken your negative characteristic, focus on one every month and try to implement it throughout the month. After six months, move to the right side of the paper and try to implement one of the strengthening actions per month. At the end of the year, examine your progress. Celebrate your success. If necessary, start all over again in the new year with two other characteristics you'd like to strengthen or weaken.

Carol

Ibegan to be a worrier in earnest at around age six. That's when my best friend, Carol, got cancer. Many painful months later, she died. I know now, over three decades later, how an adult experiences the death of a child. But with Carol I experienced her illness and death as a child. It is a uniquely devastating perspective, and that imprint has stayed with me all my life. So have the small, sharp icicles of fear it left in my heart, soul and mind.

That child I was so many years ago would be able to describe only in fragments what she knew and felt. She still lives in me, and so I know what she would say.

"Today, Carol couldn't come out and ride on the swing with me," the little girl I once was would report. "It's a big enough swing. I could have held her on my lap to make sure she wouldn't fall because she's so little now, like a tiny bird. But she's too sick today. We used to swing all the time. I wonder when we will again.

"Carol's father's fruit trees are so full they're dropping fruit on the ground. I like the plums and pears the best. We have a basketful at home. I wonder if Carol still can eat them, all sliced up in a bowl. We used to have so much fun running through the garden and the woods behind her house. Our mothers wouldn't let us out of their sight, but it was such a big yard we could pretend we were in another country. It's not much fun without her. I wonder when she'll come outside again. I think it's warm enough now. She could wear a sweater.

"Mom was going to take me to see Carol today, but she had to go back to the hospital in New Haven yesterday. I don't like how the place looks. I've waited for Mom there when she goes to see Carol. I can't go up. They think I'm too little. I wonder when Carol will come home. I wonder if she hurts. Does she cry? Is she scared? Everyone keeps saying she looks like a little angel. I wonder if she feels like a little angel. Can she see the other angels yet?

"We went to Carol's house Christmas afternoon. Everyone was so happy. Carol was home, lying on the couch with her big smile. She looked like a little porcelain doll, but she had her Happy Face on. Everyone was so excited she was there. Her aunts and her mother sang and played the organ and danced around the Christmas tree to make her laugh. She did. We sang Christmas carols for Carol! She smiled and laughed her quiet, snorting little giggle. She didn't eat anything. She sleeps in a bed that's like a big crib now. She doesn't get to sleep upstairs with her sisters and the hamsters anymore.

"Mom says Carol has died and is in heaven. I don't believe her, but maybe I do. Look at how hard Mom's crying. It's true. No. I don't believe her, but maybe I do. There are people all over the place. They talk in quiet voices, but they talk and talk and talk. The days all run together with the voices. I hear one thing over and over again. 'It's a blessing,' the voices say. What does that mean? How could it be a blessing? I don't understand. When will I see Carol again? Is she finally, really, a little angel? Can I see her at night in the sky? Did her mother want to go with her? Where is heaven? Is Carol sitting on God's lap? Does she miss her mother? Will I die, too? Do I have to die before I can see Carol again? Will I get really sick and hurt all over, too? Will people cry? Will Mom miss me?"

That seven-year-old child's questions were never answered because, of course, she never asked them. I was a child who would rather watch than speak, and over the years I have learned what I needed to know mostly by watching. But I have carried around those unasked and unanswered questions always, and they have shaped my life. I'm only beginning to discover that faith does not offer answers, only comfort. I want to learn how to embrace that comfort. I'm still trying.

Prayer

Loving Father, I've carried so many questions around for so long. My life hasn't always been easy. Teach me to lay down my burdens and lift up my arms to your embrace.

Exercise

Is there a child in your life who may be anxious? Kids today have so many more worrisome issues than children of even a generation ago. From watching terrorist attacks on television to dealing with peer pressure, youth violence and addiction—the list is staggering. Arrange to spend a morning or afternoon with a youngster in your life: perhaps your own child, a niece, nephew, younger sibling, neighbor or godchild. If the child is very young, offer to baby-sit (giving the parents a much needed break) or take an older child on an outing. Concentrate on being a good listener during your time together. General questions about school, sports and hobbies are fine, but the important thing is for the child to know you are open to listening. If the child expresses a concern or fear, be reassuring and supportive. If the situation is serious enough to warrant following up, do so. But your main objective should be to try to see life through the child's eyes. Let the youngster know that your door—and your mind—is open to him or her in the future.

The Rock

Fear tries to separate us from God. It cannot truly succeed, of course, but that doesn't always stop us from feeling that it has. We may become so overwhelmed with worry that we stop trusting that God has everything in hand. We give fear that power. For people troubled by constant worry, this happens daily. We often can't see through the haze of anxiety to discern God's loving presence. That doesn't mean God's not there. It just means that we've temporarily closed our eyes. All we have to do is lift up our faces and look.

But sometimes we feel inadequate to make even that small effort. We may feel we've hurt God by our mistrust. We may feel unworthy to ask God's help in driving away our dread and shame. We may even perceive God as a Punishing Parent who could never forgive our many mistakes. That's when we should remember that God has provided us the best possible model of how love conquers all fear.

That model is Saint Peter—the head of the apostles, the "rock" on which the church was built.

Is there a more worried figure in all the New Testament than Peter? He is the embodiment of fear. He worries about every conceivable thing. He worries about paying taxes. He worries about how Jesus could stay on the mountain after he's been transfigured. He worries about walking on the water at Jesus' invitation—*even as he's doing it*—and his worry literally sinks him. He worries that Jesus is talking too much about his impending crucifixion. He worries about Jesus washing his feet.

He worries so much that he denies Jesus three times.

But Jesus not only forgives Peter, he makes him the leader of the fledgling church. He gives this worried, anxious man the mantle for the Way that would revolutionize the entire world.

Peter: the fearful one, the worrier, the one who "put his foot in it" every chance he got!

To me, this is no coincidence. It was not a bit of capriciousness or whimsy on Jesus' part. He knew Peter's weaknesses, and yet he selected him from the start: "You are Peter, and on this rock I will build my church."

I don't think that Jesus selected Peter in spite of his fearfulness but because of it. Not only was Peter to lead the church in his lifetime, he was to become an eternal living lesson for all of us. Peter worried and worried and worried, unto the despairing point of denial. And God forgave and forgave and forgave, unto the pinnacle of love.

The next time fear overwhelms you or turns you away from God and you are too ashamed or dismayed with yourself to turn back, remember Peter. Then gird yourself with courage and throw yourself into the water, even if you are sure you will sink. Your Lord is waiting to catch you.

Prayer

Jesus, sometimes I feel I should hide my face from you. I fear I've disappointed you over and over again with my worrying and lack of trust in your love for me. Help me remember that Peter, your beloved friend and chosen leader, was as human and pitiful as I. Give me the courage to run, unashamed, into your open arms.

Exercise

Do you worry that your fears have somehow separated you from God? Has your worrying led you to a place where you didn't quite trust God to take care of you? Have you been too anxious to seek God's presence? Do you think you might not be worthy of God's loving attention? Remember that after Peter denied Jesus three times, Jesus gave him the opportunity to recant that denial three times following the Resurrection. Three times Jesus asked Peter if he loved him, and three times Peter replied forcefully in the affirmative. Go to a quiet place and kneel. Think of a specific time that your fear led you away from God. Now, "recant" that separation by repeating three times in prayer, "I trust you, Lord. I trust you, Lord. I trust you, Lord." If and when that particular worry comes up again, recall this prayer of trust and thrust the anxiety away from you. It has lost its power to come between you and God.

What, Me Worry?

"Isn't it beautiful?" I gnashed my teeth and choked back my scathing response. I was so sick of winter I could scream, yet here she was, talking about how beautiful the latest snowfall looked in the yard and on the trees and hedges. It might have been beautiful in December right before Christmas, I thought to myself, *but it was March twenty-eighth!* Snow had ceased being beautiful two months ago in what had to be the longest winter of my life.

But not to her. To her, it was just a lovely spring snowstorm. Sure, I thought, *she* doesn't have to worry about driving in the stuff. *Her* husband doesn't have to make a long commute every day, regardless of how icy and dangerous the roads. *Her* anxiety-busting daily walk wasn't ruined by the weather. *She* was not anxiously watching the tides, wary of the predicted flooding. All *she* had to do was sit in her lovely, well-kept little home and look out onto the heavy wet snow clinging prettily to the budding trees.

She gazed at me, smiling, knowing just what I was thinking. "Dear," she said in her small, raspy voice, "what exactly do you have to worry about?"

My anxiety gave way to sheepishness. What, indeed? My tiny, ninety-year-old friend had asked a simple question, but she was wise enough to know the implications. She knew what thoughts her words would provoke in me.

Mary didn't have to worry about driving in the snow because illness and age had rendered her legally blind and unable to drive anymore. This active woman who had visited cities all over the world couldn't leave her house anymore without help. She wasn't worrying about her husband commuting on winter roads because he had died thirty years ago. She wasn't worried about the tides because she'd had to sell her big, comfortable home by the sea when she could no longer climb stairs. Her daily calming exercise was not impacted by the snow because the only exercise she wanted or needed was to walk through rooms filled with her memories and photos of her family and friends.

Did Mary have any worries at all? Not really. Of course, she did wonder what I looked like, since she couldn't see my features. And she couldn't visit her old college friend in California because she couldn't be away from her doctors for more than a day or two. She never worried about food since someone always seemed to bring her something when she didn't feel up to cooking. She was very proud of the "alarm" she wore around her neck, since pressing it would immediately summon help if she needed it. She was a little concerned about the library sending her more books-on-tape than she could listen to, since she didn't want anyone else to miss out. The light was out on her front porch, but she didn't go out at night anyway so it really didn't make any difference. She'd broken her wrist this past Christmas when she went out to cut some greens off a pine tree, but that had pretty much healed by now. She hoped her many medications wouldn't cause any adverse reactions, but she thought she'd probably be fine.

Yep, all she had to do was sit in her lovely, well-kept home and look out upon the lovely spring snowfall. And ask me the very important question: "What exactly do *you* have to worry about?"

Prayer

Wise Lord, help me see the "big picture" when my silly little worries threaten to overwhelm me. Let me understand that my problems are nothing compared to those some people live with. Help me recognize the wondrous models you've provided me and give me the wisdom to emulate them.

Exercise

Someone once made a very sage observation: *No matter how bad you think you have it, someone else has it much worse.* An addendum might be: *And they might well be handling their significant burdens much better than you're handling your little fears!* Think about it. You probably know someone like this: someone who's lost a loved one, lives with serious illness, struggles as a single parent. Forget your own worries for a while and focus on this person. Pray for him or her. Call or send a card. Visit if you can. Bring a gift, a meal, flowers. And learn from your "role model" what it means to have courage and faith. Then ask yourself: What *do* I really have to worry about?

Almost as Hard
as Despair

Internationally known Christian writer Marion Bond West survived the early death of her husband and managed to struggle foward, raising her four children by herself and going on to write about her experience and faith in *The Nevertheless Principle.* Years later, she met and married Gene Acuff, a sensitive, joyful man who brought love, renewal and laughter into her life.

It was only then that Marion understood the meaning of something she'd read long ago and nearly forgotten: "Joy can be almost as hard as despair."

This is a comment that rings painfully true for those of us living in the maw of fear. When fear is a constant companion, joy takes on the aspect of a stranger. It becomes something unfamiliar and, in the cruelest ironic sense, something to be feared. It is all but impossible to welcome joy into a life filled with anxiety, but sometimes joy manages to find a way in anyway. And when joy does burst into our fearful lives, it can seem like an intruder.

As Marion discovered, the agony (though not the ecstacy) of joy can be sharpest when it comes on the heels of despair or extreme anxiety. Joy can appear to be our enemy if we are accustomed to keeping our heads down and our feet shuffling along on the path of fear. Having spent our lives avoiding the prospect of joy, we're stunned and dismayed when it manages to invade our lives unbidden. Once we recognize it—and that in itself may take time—our first reaction will likely be one of suspicion: What is joy doing here? How did it get in? Who *let* it in? Where did it come from? Where will it reside in my life since it has no resting place or room of its own?

When we realize—despite our best efforts—that joy has somehow gotten past our defenses, a whole different set of concerns surface: How do we live with it? How do we accommodate it? Can it be made comfortable? What does it mean in the context of daily life? How will it impact our future?

If we do get to the point where we can accommodate joy, and especially if we ever progress to the place where we can not only accommodate but coexist with it (and even steal a few moments of secret pleasure in its presence), then comes the most excruciating question of all for a worrier: What if joy goes away again?

Because it will. Unquestionably, joy comes and goes. Such is its nature. So when joy fades—or disappears completely for a time—what happens to us worriers who have finally learned to accommodate and even enjoy it?

That's when we must remember that joy is not fickle in its travels. It may come and go, but it is much more likely to return to a place where it is wanted. Joy may be fleeting, but it is not capricious. It recognizes a friend and rushes into the embrace of anyone who welcomes it. It goes where it is acknowledged and appreciated and loved. It goes where it is beckoned. It returns to those who yearn for it and expect it and keep a place ready for it and celebrate its return.

Of course, so does fear.

Prayer

Creator of all joy, help me to welcome your gift into my life as often as you send it. Help me not to squander the myriad opportunities you offer to live with joy. Help keep me from allowing fear to drive it away. Let joy work in my life to banish fear.

Exercise

Think back to the last time you rejected joy. It might have been this morning when you hurried your child through a good-bye hug. It might have been yesterday when a coworker wanted you to celebrate his or her recent engagement. It might have been last Christmas when you took the decorations down early. Chances are, you'll have many possibilities to choose from. Select one and imagine yourself reliving that opportunity. Remember precisely why you chose to ignore joy: not enough time, too frivolous, too ethereal, too silly, too unfamiliar, too disruptive, too scary. Then, picture yourself welcoming joy instead of turning it away. Think about what you could have done to entice joy to stay with you as long as possible. Promise yourself that you will welcome joy at the very next opportunity, no matter how frightening or inconvenient the prospect may be.

No More
Vegetables First!

My husband has a habit that always puzzled me. He always eats first what he likes most. If he has a number of items on his plate, he'll always dig enthusiastically into the food he most relishes. He'll occasionally make a foray into the other selections, but he focuses happily on his favorite. It's the same with desserts. If I return from the bakery with several different treats, he'll always choose his favorite, leaving the less desired sweet for "tomorrow night." He lives his whole life this way. If he has a number of weekend tasks to tackle, he'll always start Saturday morning with the one that most interests him or the one he knows he'll most enjoy.

I, on the other hand, have spent my whole life doing the hard stuff first, getting it over with. When I have several writing assignments, I invariably tackle the most difficult one first—even if it has a later deadline. When I have a number of publishers and editors to phone, I force myself to first dial up the one most likely to give me a hard time or bad news. I open bills before letters. I always eat my vegetables first. I never open the best flavor of ice cream until the other kind is finished. Even as a kid on Easter, I always saved my Cadbury eggs for last, after the malted milk balls and jellybeans were long gone.

To me, this is just normal operating procedure, the best way to get through life. It took me years with my husband to realize that my way *isn't* the best way. Indeed, my way is the worrying way—the way that denies spontaneity and joy, the way that breeds anxiety and fear in the shadows along the path.

This revelation came at the end of one particular weekend. It was late Sunday night, just before dinner. As usual, all the household chores that my beloved enjoyed were done. Left un-done was the broken kitchen cabinet, which meant that I'd continue to be faced with the same disconcerting sight I'd been staring at for weeks: a gaping open cabinet with its array of mismatched plates, dishes and mugs displayed for the world—and most importantly, me—to observe. Just the sight of it made me feel disorganized and sloppy. I work so hard to keep chaos at bay, I thought, couldn't I at least have cabinets that shut out the odds and ends of life?

Steam must have been blowing from my ears as I went in search of my dearest, the ranting words already on my tongue. I found him standing on the porch in the twilight, looking over the nearby harbor as the early moon rose. One majestic sailboat was gliding in toward its mooring. The mast captured the lights from the shore as they twinkled on the dock. When he turned to beckon me out to join him, his face was filled with delight and anticipation of my pleasure.

I gulped. And then I joined him.

Much later, when I'd managed to swallow my guilt for near-ly ruining a wonderful evening over such small anxieties, I forced myself to consider just how much joy I was missing in my determination to first tackle all of life's "grim realities." Was there any real benefit to postponing pleasure, even the simple pleasures of watching a moon rise or eating a favorite food? Or had that habit of deferring joy simply become my way of allowing worry and negativism to reign? Was there any point to finishing all the unpleasant tasks in life, if that meant I never got to the lovely parts? If worrisome matters continued to consume all my attention, would I finally lose all access to the joyous, peaceful aspects of life?

What's a better way to end a weekend: tying myself up in knots over all that I hadn't gotten done, or enjoying all that God had done already?

Prayer

Lord, help me to avoid focusing on the difficult or tedious aspects of life. So often I imprison myself in a cell of negativity. Free me, Lord. Help me learn to confront life's challenges without ignoring life's pleasures...pleasures that you have provided.

Exercise

Think about someone you know who always seems to take life easy. Picture that person in your mind's eye. Close you eyes and examine how you "see" that person. Are you critical of the "happy-go-lucky" nature? Do you harbor secret disdain for such an easy-going attitude? Do you consider him or her lazy or a layabout? It's time to ask God to help you change your perception. Try to see the person as God does. For instance, where you see silliness, God may hear a song of praise in laughter. Where you see laziness, God may see a pause to quietly pray. Where you see aimlessness, God may see someone searching for the best path to the divine presence. Now, open your eyes and try to act like a child of God. Smile or laugh at a full moon, the stars, a newly blooming tree or flower, or even children playing. Try to incorporate this practice into your life on a daily basis, even if it means not eating your vegetables first!

The Bright Side

"If God gives you lemons...make lemonade!" "Every cloud has a silver lining!" "The glass is half-full, not half-empty!" "Don't forget to stop and smell the roses!" "Hey, look on the bright side!"

Everyone's heard these optimistic exclamations often enough, but Gretchen, the busy self-employed and always anxious mom, had heard them once too often. "It was getting to the point that every time I turned around, someone was spouting some trite saying," she groused. "Everything in my life was going wrong, but no one wanted to hear it. Did I get any sympathy? No! All I got were these ridiculous little bromides, ad nauseam."

Gretchen recalled how her own mother was the worst offender: "Here I was going to her for understanding, maybe even a little pity, and Mom's chirping this stuff at me as if reading from a book of cheery sayings. My middle daughter, Kate, was sick with mononucleosis; I was spending all my working time taking care of her; our health insurance wasn't going to cover all the medicines she needed; I worried about her being held back a year in school; and the stupid car was going in for an overhaul with no loaner in the offing from the garage. And here's Mom, acting like I'm on a picnic or something.

"I'd really had it one day. She was supposed to be bringing us some groceries, and instead of following my list specifically, she bought oranges instead of bananas. When I asked her why, in what was probably a not very nice tone of voice, she breezily replied that the oranges were 'much brighter and sunnier to cheer you all up!' I lost it. I'd specifically asked for bananas because I wanted Kate to have the extra potassium. I all but shrieked as much to my mother. She—to her credit—just looked back at me very steadily, not upset or anything but just sort of studying me.

"Finally she said, 'Gretch, the world is not ending. You need to calm down and see that. No one's dying. Other kids have had mono and recovered just fine. You had it, for Pete's sake! Maybe it's not such a bad thing for Kate to get a breather from everything going on with her school clique now. Have you noticed how that creepy boy she was seeing isn't coming around so much? And you've always worried too much about money. Your clients aren't going anywhere, and you're not going broke in the meantime. Yes, medication is expensive, but be thankful they have such good drugs these days. And it's a good thing the mechanic found the problem with the car before you were in an accident. Someday, not so very long from now, you're going to look back on this and be proud that you got through it. Believe me. I know.'

"And she did know. My brother and I had put her through hell growing up. Whatever trouble there was to get into, we did. She'd been a single mom well before it was fashionable—or even acceptable. She must have worried about money, health care, our bratty behavior—you name it. She must have wondered if she'd ever have time for herself, if she'd be too old before she could relax and enjoy life. My life is easy compared to hers. Yet somehow she'd found the distance and the faith to look on the bright side...and give me that perspective.

"All my anger and fear seemed to drain away. I slumped onto a kitchen chair. 'Mom,' I began. But she interrupted me by coming over and putting her arms around me. 'I know,' she said, 'I know.'"

Prayer

Discerning Father, you made both the clouds and the silver linings. Teach me to see both. When darkness threatens to overwhelm me, help me see the light. Open my heart and spirit to the prospect of happy endings.

Exercise

You too can learn from Gretchen's mother. Consider a situation in your life that you've perceived as bleak or particularly distressing. Now change your assumptions about it. Look for the bright side. For example, if you dread an upcoming "command performance" event with family, in-laws, friends or work, try to look at it differently. Could you make a good impression rather than just "get through it"? If you're nervous about what to say, why not pre-select appropriate topics to discuss? Maybe there will be good food and drink to enjoy. There might be someone interesting whom you don't expect to see. If all else fails, remind yourself how great you'll feel when it's all over and done with, and promise yourself a special reward when it is. Now go and approach the situation with your new "bright side" perspective.

Love an Optimist

Every worrier has optimists in his or her life. Unfortunately, many of us deliberately dismiss these folks instead of embracing them. We may be annoyed by their cheerful attitude in the midst of our self-styled suffering. We may not want anyone to disturb our studied pessimism. We may be already addicted to anxiety and worry, unable to lay down the burden of fear. Change is hard, even change that drives a hopeful wedge between us and anxiety. We may not think we're choosing darkness over light, but fear may already be a habit.

A great antidote to the habit of fear is the optimist—not just the optimist's perspective, but the optimist himself or herself. I've found that the very existence of someone with an attitude so diametrically opposed to mine is always a fresh and wonderful surprise. It's even better—and more effective at stunning me out of my dread—when the source is unexpected.

Our friend Tom was just such a surprise. He's also a financial advisor, so it's probably a good thing he's an optimist. Tom is usually all business, the consummate professional. He works and lives in Buffalo, New York, which is a situation I find incomprehensible. Actually, what I find incomprehensible is that he and his family *choose* to live in Buffalo. I think it's bad enough to live in Connecticut, where winter reigns for at least six months of the year and the other six months are divided between thunderstorms and hurricanes.

But Buffalo! Buffalo is a worrier's nightmare. It snows every day in Buffalo, except for maybe nine days a year. The roads are always treacherous. The airport runways are always slick. It's cold and bleak and there's disaster waiting around every corner.

At least that's how I think. Tom, however, thinks much differently.

Tom came to visit Charlie and me in Connecticut one beautiful April day, at about the time that Spring had arrived everywhere except Greenland, Iceland, the Arctic...and Buffalo. Tom, to my amazement, missed Buffalo. He told me, "This is the best time of year at home, when it starts getting light later in the day. Did you know that at the end of the day Buffalo has a few more minutes of light than the rest of the Eastern time zone? It's because we're right on the western edge of the zone, and it's especially noticeable in late spring. That means the sun shines each evening just a few minutes longer in Buffalo than on the rest of the eastern seaboard. That's something I really love about living there."

I was astonished. If I were Tom, I'd be thinking about my kids riding in school buses on slippery roads, my wife worrying at home while I was stuck at the airport in a storm, my staff not being able to make it to work in a blizzard, the frozen dampness for such an interminable stretch of every year. That's what I'd be thinking about. But that's not what Tom is thinking about. Tom's thinking about those few extra moments of sunlight.

Prayer

Lord, thank you for putting sunny souls and light hearts in my path. Help me to appreciate them more. When fear would drive me away from them, please turn me back. When worry would lock my arms tightly at my side, teach me to open them in welcome.

Exercise

There are probably a number of optimists in your life, though in the past you may have too easily dismissed their contributions. Make a list of four people you know who tend to look on the bright side. If you've ever let your fears or irritations turn you away from these people, offer a prayer asking God to forgive you. On each of the next four Mondays, call one of these people. (Put it in your calendar as an appointment you must keep.) Tell the person you've been feeling discouraged about aspects of your life and ask for their perspective. Listen with an open heart. Absorb their words and advice. Thank them for their generosity. For the rest of the day, let their optimism stay firmly in your mind and try to keep it there as you go forward.

There You Are

Icouldn't believe my luck when I saw the cottage in Key West. It was absolutely perfect: neat, clean, brand new and perfectly sized for a single woman. There was even an electrical outlet by the door so I could plug in my computer and sit on the small, homey porch as I wrote. I'd be able to watch the passing colorful parade of humanity that gives the city its international reputation. A sliding glass door opened onto an overgrown garden where geckos cavorted, darting in and out of sight as if they were playing some secret game of hide and seek.

The rooms I had reserved months ago on the island hadn't worked out, and the fact that I'd found this extraordinary place in just a few hours during the busiest season of the year was almost too good to be true. It most certainly wasn't the kind of luck I'd become accustomed to. It was, I'm sure, a blessing. Once I made sure they had my check in hand, I ventured to ask my landlords how the cottage had come to be available. They told me that a young woman had recently leased it for a year, but she had gone back to her home in mainland Florida after only a few weeks. Amazed, I asked why.

She had been planning to move to Key West for some time, they said. She was in her twenties and had even found a job before she moved in. She'd not been having an easy time of it in her Florida hometown. College had not gone well. She'd gotten involved with the wrong crowd, lost a job or two. There were health issues. When she'd come to Key West for a short break, she'd fallen in love with the island. Here, at last, she could be free of all that plagued her at home. No one would be looking over her shoulder. She'd make new, exciting friends. Naturally, her physical and emotional health would be restored immediately. She'd leased the cottage at first sight. Key West would be the answer to all her problems.

Well, not exactly. She soon found she didn't like her new job so well and wasn't sure she could do it. It was hard to work in a place where it seemed that everyone else was playing. Her health didn't clear up right away either, but then everyone in Key West did too much eating and drinking, so why should she abstain? And the friends and folks at home who'd plagued her so? She found she missed them. The few people she'd met on the island were shallow and selfish. She felt confused, without direction and, eventually, miserable. My landlords had graciously let her out of the lease, knowing it was not going to work out for any of them in the long run.

I felt sorry for this woman, although we'd never met. I even empathized a little. When your life is full of problems and worries, it's hard to resist the lure of a new and enticing place: Surely everything will be different there; surely all your dilemmas and fears are due to *where* you are and not *who* you are. It was easy for me, also enamored of Key West, to understand why she might feel that way.

Of course, this is never the case. As a friend of mine who appreciates irony always says: "Wherever you go, there you are." It is a wise and wry commentary on the human condition—and piercingly true, as my Key West predecessor had discovered. A new and exciting environment can certainly provide diversion. It can pique your interest and get you excited about life again. It may offer new and intriguing job and relationship prospects. But it can't change who you are.

A person living with fear in cold, gray Caribou, Maine, is going to bring those same fears to hot, bright Key West, Florida. It may take a while for them to show up in the sun, but they'll be there, hiding in the shadows and waiting for their chance to surface. We who are fearful must live where we stand, and confront our fears in that very place. We must deliberately act to recognize them, identify them and shed them. Otherwise, we might find ourselves schlepping them around the world, with no place "good enough" to leave them behind.

Prayer

God of all places, I carry my fear with me
wherever I go. I delude myself that maybe I'll be
able to put it down "somewhere." Give me the
courage to put it down here...and now.

Exercise

Put on the oldest, rattiest pair of shoes, slippers or sneakers you own. Wear them as you go through the first hour of your day. Then, take them off. Leave them in the middle of the floor where you can see them and maybe even trip over them for the rest of the day. Let the old shoes represent your fear. Put on another pair of shoes and go about your day, leaving your tattered old shoes—and your fears—behind, at least for a day. Notice how much lighter and sharper you feel each time you walk away.

A Day in a Life

Cathy, self-avowed world-class worrier, decided to keep track of just how much time she dithered away on her fears and anxieties during any one day. She expected to be slightly dismayed with the results, hoping that would motivate her to work on loosening fear's grip. As it turned out, the little experiment left her more than dismayed. She was stunned.

"I knew I wasted time on worrying, but actually keeping track of how much was a real shocker," she reports. "I wrote down what I worried about, why I was worried about it, and how much time I spent worrying. When I read the list, I was really embarrassed. It was sort of like telling the doctor you can't figure out why you aren't losing weight since you don't 'eat much at all.' The doctor tells you to keep a careful list of every single thing you eat in a twenty-four-hour period. You do that, but then you don't want to turn in the list! It's such a glaring record of how much you really *do* eat! That's exactly how I felt as I read over my worry list."

Here's Cathy's official "dread diary" for one bright, sunny Wednesday:

1. Worried about whether my husband had remembered his cell phone; kept calling until I reached him—fifteen minutes;
2. Worried about whether my daughter had studied enough for her SATs; badgered her about it; fought when she responded snippily; stewed; apologized; lectured her on the importance of a good college and asked her to please study; continued to worry off and on all day—total one hour;

3. Worried about whether I should wear sunscreen for my hour-long bike ride; watched the sun go in and out; finally decided just to wear a hat but started worrying again when the sun came out brightly mid-ride—twenty minutes;
4. Worried about whether my mother would be upset if I didn't phone her until tomorrow—ten minutes (probably as long as we would have talked);
5. Worried about whether to buy Bosc pears, which looked good but had sticky labels all over them that would peel off the skin when I tried to remove them for washing—three minutes;
6. Worried about not yet getting the results from my annual mammogram—forty-five minutes;
7. Worried about whether my husband was eating well during this crunch time at work and whether he would be home for dinner or work late or attend a retirement party—twenty minutes;
8. Worried that the women in the office where I work were talking about me (since things suddenly got silent when I walked into work this afternoon); worried about whether it (whatever *it* was) would impact my status with my employer—thirty minutes;
9. Worried about whether we'd have enough money for a two-week vacation or if we'd have to cut it down to eleven days—thirty minutes, including calculator time;
10. Worried about the nation using the federal death penalty (for the first time in several decades)—one hour;
11. Worried whether I was praying in a way that would get God's attention; worried whether I was missing some directive or message from him—twenty-five minutes;
12. Worried about my sore knee and whether it would keep me from the bike race on Saturday; worried about whether to call the doctor and ask for a referral or just take aspirin and wait it out—thirty minutes;
13. Worried that I'd left the iron on; drove all the way back to the house after I was halfway to soccer to pick up my son—twenty minutes.

When Cathy read the list at the end of the day, she realized she had spent over six hours worrying and that "there was really nothing I could do about any of these things. Worrying about them hadn't changed anything at the end of the day. It wasn't as if I'd taken any positive action to actually *alter* these circumstances. In most cases, there was no positive action to take. It was a complete waste.

"The whole exercise really stopped me short. Other than the iron—which wasn't even on—I hadn't resolved a single issue. I'd started the list as sort of a lark, but it wasn't at all amusing anymore. I started thinking about all the things I could have done with those six hours: enjoy my bike ride, read, talk to my kids, have lunch with my husband, fix a gourmet meal from scratch, even just watch TV. For that matter, I could have rented and watched three full-length movies! I think for the first time I saw how fear ruled my life—and ruled *out* so much in my life. It was not a pretty sight."

Fear can be an ugly thing. But seeing it clearly—in all it's ugliness—is an important step toward eradicating it.

Prayer

> *Patient God, I squander so much of every precious day you give me on worrying. Please forgive me! Help me to recognize the many disguises fear will use to creep in and control my life.*

Exercise

S tarting tomorrow when you awaken, keep your own "dread diary" for the next twenty-four hours. Be honest and inclusive. Don't forget to record any time you spend tossing and turning with worry at night. At the end of the period, add up the amount of time you spent being anxious and fearful. Divide the time by four so that you have a period that is one-quarter of your worrying time for one day. Every day for the next week, spend that amount of time—one-quarter of the time you wasted in fear—with God. How you give this time back to God is up to you: meditate, pray, go to church, attend a spiritual program, read the Bible or other faith-based literature, write God a poem or story, or talk to God as you exercise or work out. Let a faith action replace your fear...at least some of it!

Everything Has Changed

When I learned I had malignant melanoma, I had just turned thirty-six and was in perfect health...or so I thought.

My extraordinary doctor called me on a Friday night...and scheduled me for surgery on Monday. Two weeks later he found and removed a similar melanoma. Fortunately (blessedly), they were both in the earliest stage and no more have been found. Every six months I have a skin checkup and sometimes a biopsy to catch anything that looks suspicious.

So not much in my life has really changed.

Except that everything has changed.

At thirty-six years, two months and five days, I considered myself invincible. At thirty-six years, two months and *six* days, I was the most vulnerable person in the world. The word *malignant* burns itself into the brain like a smoking brand. Even when the disease is driven from the body, the brand remains. From the moment I heard the word, my confidence in my health—and my ability to gauge my health—was shattered. The melanoma had been a complete surprise: I'd agreed to see the doctor only because my mother wanted me to have a skin check. As a family we'd been sun-lovers, but I was olive skinned and dark haired. Hey, I'd never even had poison ivy! No worries, right?

Wrong. Indeed, every conceivable worry came rushing into the breathless breach that had been ripped open by the diagnosis. Though a born worrier, I'd never before thought much about my own health. I'd been young, strong, brave...arrogant. I'd gone wherever I wanted to go without fear for my well-being. Now I felt like "damaged goods." I began to see myself as part of a cautious shadow world, cringing at every new sound and movement. My confidence retreated as fearsome questions charged forward.

How had I missed this potentially deadly thing lurking in my very own body? What signs had I ignored? Was I still missing, still ignoring, something vital: What was this pain? Where did that ache come from? How did I get that bruise? Why was this flu taking so long to go away? Were these new headaches because of tension...or something else?

Five years later, my fears are somewhat more predictable, but I've never regained that sense of confidence that everything's OK. Simple pains and viruses can still send me into a tailspin. I can't afford to dismiss anything. I don't dare.

Everything seems more important, more weighty, than before. I am so much more aware of time...and love.

Disease shakes the very foundation of a life. Faith makes recovery—physical, emotional and spiritual—possible, but recovery does not mean a return to life as it was before. And that may not be a bad thing...though it certainly feels like a bad thing at times.

I am reminded of a woman who survived breast cancer. A local newspaper reported her participation in a breast cancer awareness event, presenting her as someone who was "grateful for cancer." To her everlasting credit, she wrote a strong, intelligent letter to the paper gently correcting that impression: She was not grateful for cancer. She was grateful for her recovery, for the people who'd made the journey with her, for the direction her life had taken.

She was so right. No one is grateful for disease. But faith can weave the disease, and the recovery, into the pattern of one's life without shredding the tapestry. (Though the tapestry will surely feel shredded for some time!) I have had to learn a new way of living. I'm still learning. I have had to learn to stay very still and breathe in God's presence slowly and deeply when fear assaults me, as it still does. I have had to learn that I never really had the control I thought I had. I have had to learn that the greatest part of recovery is understanding that *full* recovery—as in a return to life before—is not possible. I have had to learn that something richer, something more complex, may be forged in this fire. I have had to learn to trust myself again. I have learned that none of this is possible unless I trust God.

Prayer

Compassionate Father, your mercies are innumerable. Your kindness abounds. Your strength is eternal. I have learned that you are all I have. Help me to survive that knowledge. Help me to flourish in my recovery.

Exercise

Have you experienced a shock strong enough to derail your life? Do you feel disconnected or even cut off from everything you thought to be true? Are you anxious and confused about what you need to hold onto and what you need to discard? Jesus, crucified, must have felt all that and more. And yet he embraced the experience because it would forge a new order. He did not blame God; rather, he asked God to be with him throughout his agony. After Jesus' crucifixion and resurrection, nothing would ever be the same. Find or buy for yourself a small cross. You may even make one by gluing two nails together. Carry or wear your cross at all times as you survive and recover from your shock or disease. Consider it a source of strength. When you feel especially fearful or disoriented, hold your cross in your hand and ask God to help you through this process. You may not even know the final outcome yet. Take a deep breath and accept that.

Always and in All Ways

"I am with you always," Jesus assured those gathered on the mountain just before he ascended into heaven. With these words, he made one of the most comforting promises ever recorded. Think about what it truly means to have Jesus always, to have him for company and succor—no matter what happens, no matter where we go, no matter how solitary our lives may seem. It means *we're not alone!* Not only are we not alone, we have with us the *best possible* companion and helper. How could anyone ask for more?

And yet, Jesus' final affirmation may indeed mean something even more. In promising to be with us always, he meant forever: that is, unto and through eternity. It may well be that he also meant "in all ways." The possibilities of this kind of presence are wondrously endless: Jesus in a breathtaking sunrise, Jesus in a spectacular sunset, Jesus in the laughter of your child, Jesus in the tears of a child you pass on the street, Jesus in an abundant feast, Jesus in a deliberate fast, Jesus in the triumph of a friend, Jesus in the persecution of a homeless person, Jesus in the blooming dogwood tree, Jesus in the dying rose, Jesus in the vast ocean, Jesus in the desert.

Jeff, a professor and world traveler, takes the concept of Jesus "in all ways" very seriously. And while his travels give Jeff myriad opportunities to find Jesus, he most often thinks of friends when it comes to seeing Jesus "in all ways."

"When I think of the many ways Jesus can be with me, I always come back to my friends," he explains. "What better way to experience Jesus, the ultimate friend, than through your own friends? I think Jesus touches me often and blessedly through my friends.

"I can't begin to count the times it happens. There was the time that our neighbor, Kira, came bursting into a faculty meeting to tell me my wife had gone into labor a month early. I was too shaken to even drive to the hospital, so Kira drove like a madwoman and got me there before our son was born. Then there was the time that Jack, a colleague at my college, gave me his place on a working academic tour of the Middle East because he'd been there and I hadn't. And always there's my editor, who fights for me every time a manuscript of mine doesn't precisely fit into the publisher's plans.

"There are also the friends I hardly know, through whom Jesus also comes to me. There's the lady at church who welcomed me into what was a very close-knit parish. All she does is smile and shake my hand vigorously every week, but she's made me feel as if someone cares that I'm there. There's the young man at the deli where my wife and I spend the 'lion's share' of our discretionary income. He always has a kind word for us and often puts aside portions of our favorite foods. The youngsters (well, they seem like youngsters to me) who run the video store never fail to be courteous and pleasant. They give us running reviews of every new film and always ask how we liked our most recent selection.

"Perhaps the friends who most truly make Jesus known to me 'in all ways' are the friends who help me with faith. These are the people who know my worries, my fears, my doubts. Some of them have their own anxieties, so it's not like someone sitting there pontificating and giving me all the answers. But they join me in seeking faith and understanding. We discuss our fears. We support each other in difficult times. When necessary, we read each other the 'riot act.' I guess the most important thing we do is learn together how to pray and what faith and discipleship really mean."

Prayer

Jesus, Lord and Brother, open my eyes to the "all ways" you are with me, especially through the people in my life. Help me to feel your presence in them.

Exercise

Reach out to Jesus in the people in your life. Every day for the next week, contact one person who has helped you, taught you, shared with you, or simply loved you. It needn't be someone who is regularly in your life now. In fact, think especially about your past and people you've lost consistent touch with. They might appreciate hearing from you even more than your neighbor or best friend. Check your address book, Rolodex or Christmas card list. You may call, write or even e-mail the individual. As you do, remind yourself—and perhaps that person—of both the fearful and joyful times you might have shared. Think about what you learned from this friend. Tell the person how much you value him or her. Later, pray for this person's welfare and thank God for bringing this friend into your life. After the week is over, try to continue this practice at least once a month. Perhaps you will become one of the "all ways" Jesus comes into someone else's life.

Choose to Change

For anxious souls like me, the path from fear and worldly concerns to faith does not seem easily trod. That's because conscious change is *not* easy. It takes will. It takes effort. It takes a belief that the destination is wonderful enough to endure a journey that may be less than wonderful. Jesus himself warned us to beware of the fruitless path, the rocky ground, the painful thorns along the way.

But the simple decision to change is, in itself, a joyful rejection of the fear-filled apathy that can trap our soul. So the decision *to* change is, indeed, the first step *in* change. It's also probably the easiest.

For although God has given souls practical as well as spiritual opportunities through which to heal and change, at first glance all of them may seem frightening. That is the nature of change: It requires embracing something that is not familiar, not necessarily comfortable. One man who found himself increasingly paralyzed by worry had a very typical reaction when given the opportunity to change his anxious behavior through therapy. With no trace of irony at all, he replied, "Oh, I don't know. All those appointments. All that talking about myself. It's just one more thing to worry about."

The process of change is not easy. Indeed, as the worried gentleman demonstrated, the journey itself can initially bring out even worse fears. Marion Bond West would say that Satan doesn't want the soul to reach the destination of faith and makes the trip seem impossible by "ratcheting up the fear factor." Whether it's Satan—or as Ms. Claire, the librarian, would suggest, the ego—there is a strong, dark force that resists the soul's efforts to reject fear and embrace faith. Yet, regardless of how daunting the wave of fear that crests at our first attempts to change, we can ride that wave into calm waters by a trusting act of will.

For the fearful soul, the catalysts that can motivate change are many. There are wonderful therapists who can help: psychiatrists, psychologists, social workers and counselors, women and men religious, priests, ministers, rabbis and spiritual advisors. Some of us find freedom from stress and anxiety in alternative therapies: massage, physical therapy, music therapy, acupuncture and aromatherapy. For others, medications prescribed by a caring, knowledgeable doctor can work wonders in clearing away anxiety.

The charismatic movement has facilitated change for a number of souls who previously believed their faith could be expressed only in a specific and often constrained manner. For others, very simple changes have inspired a new perspective: joining the church choir, volunteering to plant flowers or a garden on the church or church-school grounds, getting involved in a community-based volunteer project, or teaching Sunday School. Other change agents include meditation, yoga, regular walking or biking, swimming, joining a book or spiritual discussion group, reading inspirational books, working puzzles, or developing a calming, centering hobby like needlecraft or pottery.

The list of help that God provides is endless. God wants us to get off the barren path, reject the rocky ground and escape the thorns. This won't be easy. That's why God is there—offering every support possible.

Make the decision. Choose to change. Then take the first step—and keep going.

Prayer

Lord, help my eyes pierce the fog of fear. Let me recognize the many paths you provide to a fuller, fearless faith. Lead me to the one that's right for me and help me stay on it. Please let me feel your presence on the journey.

Exercise

Examine yourself honestly with an eye toward selecting an action that will help you move away from anxiety and toward faith. Ask yourself the following questions: What hobbies or forms of exercise do I most enjoy? Can I be trusting enough to be open in therapy? Do I experience actual panic attacks that could be alleviated with prescribed medication or a combination of medication and therapy? Do I prefer to be on my own or in a group? Am I most relaxed indoors in a more structured environment or outdoors hiking or mountain climbing? Would I prefer a traditional religious or an alternative spiritual exercise—or a program that combines the two? Answer your self-examination honestly and use the answers to shape a change program that will be specific to you and most helpful to your journey from fear to faith. Understand that anything you undertake is likely to increase your fear and anxiety at first. Resolve to maintain your program regardless of this escalation. Reject the force that would derail your efforts. Ask God for help, and know that by doing nothing more than asking you will be granted all the strength and grace you are willing to accept.

24/7/365/Eternity

It is one thing to think, hope and pray about increasing our faith. It's another thing to act. Without acting, the other things are no more than good intentions at best—and cerebral exercises at worst.

But don't panic. Active faith does not consist of a series of massive, dramatic actions. Remember that Jesus refused to jump off the tall building to prove to Satan that God loved him. Ostentation is not faith, or as one friend puts it, "Martyrdom has its own set of problems!" Faith actions should not be undertaken to prove anything to anyone...except yourself, and even that should be a quiet thing between you and God. Remember again how Jesus cautioned his disciples against the public acts and loud prayers of the scribes and Pharisees, telling them that the Father sees and rewards what is done in private.

A simple, personal, private act of faith—just between you and the Father—can be a most powerful catalyst for your journey from fear to faith. Involving a beloved friend, spouse or family member in your faith act can strengthen your own resolve and the bond between the two of you. Such an act may also bring your beloved closer to God and encourage his or her faith progress.

I learned this before I got married. In the time my husband and I had been together, my fear had grown proportionately with my love. Loving acts were often attended by a gripping fear that one day death might separate us. I'd heard that love made some people nervous, but this was ridiculous! Of course, my fears weren't always at a fever pitch—we had too much fun together for me to be miserable all the time—but they were there as often as not.

I thought and hoped and prayed about increasing my faith and decreasing my fears. But again, good intentions and cerebral exercises go only so far. I needed to focus more aggressively on God's promise of eternal life and my faith that Charlie and I will be together during eternity. And I needed small, quiet actions that I could take—with his support—to help me.

Our wedding provided the perfect opportunity. When we selected our rings, the jeweler asked if we wanted an inscription. I think she expected me to ask for the wedding date or our initials or something traditional like that. Charlie, knowing me better, probably expected me to say, "Don't bother." Instead, I asked for the inscription "24/7/365/Eternity." This was a phrase he had come up with to help ease my fears, to remind me that God had brought us together...twenty-four hours a day for seven days a week for 365 days a year, unto and through eternity. Every once in a while, one of us would say to the other, "Remember, 24/7/365/Eternity," and it was always comforting. I wanted it on our rings.

This was a small, personal, private act of faith, but now I have constantly with me the reminder of God's love and our commitment. Just looking at my ring is an action that strengthens me and pulls me up out of the morass of worry that sometimes entraps me. It reminds me that God's love for us is eternal. And my husband, who probably came up with our mantra just to soothe me, is now walking this path with me. When I ask him, "Tell me what you believe" about God, faith and sundry other spiritual matters, he laughs and says, "I believe what you believe." I think he thinks that will make life easier for him.

I have faith it will.

Prayer

Eternal Father, you give me so many opportunities to act faithfully. Thank you! Teach me to recognize and seize them no matter how small or private they may seem. Help me remember that you see and love every effort we make to move closer to you.

Exercise

Address one of your deepest fears with a small act of faith today. Don't dismiss this act because it is small. It could be profoundly meaningful to you, and therefore size and scope do not matter. Light an incense cone or stick and place it in an incense burner or clean ashtray. Let the incense represent your deep fear or worry. Watch as it burns. See your fear go up in smoke. Measure the time it takes for your fear to be dissipated. Thank God for giving you this opportunity to let your fear go, to move into the divine presence. Save the tiny ash in a container labeled with this particular worry. When your worry comes back to burden you, lift the tiny bit of ash and feel how insubstantial that fear truly is in the greater universe of God's abiding love for you.

Faith Isn't Easy

Some of my Christian friends tell me that faith is easy. I may be oversimplifying their position, but the theory seems to go something like this: You have faith, you're saved, you go to heaven. Or, as they say in Australia, "No worries." One of my Evangelical colleagues puts it this way: "Faith is like falling in love: It's simply something that happens to you—and there you are!"

Well, I guess anyone who thinks falling in love is easy probably does think faith is easy. Or perhaps it's more accurate to say that someone who finds it easy to fall in love probably will indeed find it easy to fall into faith. May God bless them for it.

For many of us, however, faith isn't easy. Loving God-the-Father-Son-and-Spirit may be easy. Talking to God may be easy. Worshiping God may be easy. Thanking God may be easy. Asking God for forgiveness may be easy. But faith is not so easy. Faith is vital, life-giving, the source of all that is good. Faith is comforting, exciting, frightening, daring, attractive, enticing, intriguing, simple, inexplicable, wondrous...and it is therefore not easy, at least to us worriers.

We live in a time when the very complexity of the world makes faith difficult. Technology brings us news of disasters, cruelties, disease, political intrigue, greed, viciousness and terrorism...all within seconds of these events occuring. We are inundated with evidence that something is seriously wrong with humanity.

How can faith stand against this barrage of evident evil?

How can faith stand in the face of recent history and current events?

How can faith stand opposite the mirror of our personal tragedies and agonies?

The answer is that faith does not stand. Faith *flows*. It is in, around, above, below and through everything. It is the flowing, living energy that binds us to the Creator. It has nothing to do with tragedy, disaster, human nature, cruelty. Faith is not part of the cause-effect chain we consistently and desperately try to forge with our questions. Faith links us to the love of God, not to the nature of humankind. Faith cannot be seen, described or blamed.

For faith is the unique life source that is not just of God nor just of humankind. It is that one shimmering entity that brings the divine within reach of the human: God gives us the grace to seek faith, but we must yearn for it if we are to grasp it. Any attempt to understand or define or justify faith is futile. Not only will that effort fail, it is pointless. What can it gain us to try to explain faith? In fact, it can only weaken that which we seek, because to explain faith is to constrain it. If we are determined to reduce faith to the human realm, we must strip it of the divine. And what does that gain us?

We must want faith so badly that we willingly let all our defenses fall away: our inquisitiveness, our driving need to know, our determination to control, our dread of the inexplicable, our lack of trust.

Faith may not be easy, but with faith everything else is. So stop questing to *know* faith and start yearning to *possess* it. That's the first step. And the last.

Prayer

Father, thank you for the gift of faith. Give me the courage to reject my human fears and worries and questions so that I may accept this precious bond with you.

Exercise

Think of your most precious possession. Perhaps it is a jewel, a piece of art, your home. Do you need to dissect every aspect of it to know how precious it is to you? Must you know every property of the jewel—what country it came from, what makes it shine, who mined it, who imported it? Must you know the age and life story of the painter, who owned the painting before you, who framed it, what material it was packed in? Must you know every person who worked on your home, what nursery seeded the first lawn, who cut the glass for the windows, who fit the gutters, what material forms the bricks in the chimney? Do you need to know every detail about a thing you possess to appreciate its full sensual and spiritual value to you? Probably not. Indeed, obsession with minutiae may detract from the whole. In the same way, faith is not precious because you know and understand its origin and every component. It is precious because you want it and need it and seek it and are fulfilled by it. And next to it, even your most precious possession will pale.

Acknowledgments

It is my hope that God guided every word of this work. Its writer had a great deal of human help as well. This book would not have been possible without the following people: Lisa Giordano, Jaye Lyon and Elaine Marie Shallenberger, my intrepid readers, who kindly bracketed their criticism with encouragement; my parents, who inspired this book; my sister, Lori Polito, who steadfastedly stands between me and the abyss of fear; Aires and Natalie Pont and Stella Cidale, my friends and mentors; Gerry Klender, who believed this book would be written before I did and brilliantly negotiated the deal that made it possible; Andrew and Julia Attaway, who lead by example; Marion Bond West and Joni Woelfel, who've taught me much about writing, faith and friendship; and Jerry and Arden Lites, whom my husband and I are blessed to have found.

To those who have helped and loved me along the way, from my dearest friends to my readers and correspondents: There are not enough pages in this book to name and thank you all. Besides, I'd worry about forgetting someone!

Finally, this book is in no small part a loving testament to my husband, Charlie, who—to my alternating consternation, astonishment and admiration—*knows no fear!* The kind of faith I work for flows easily in and through him, and for that I am eternally grateful.